Reading and Language Arts
Worksheets
Don't Grow Dendrites

Reading and Language Arts
Worksheets
Don't Grow Dendrites

20

Literacy Strategies That Engage the Brain

Marcia L. Tate

CORWIN PRESS
A SAGE Publications Company
Thousand Oaks, California

Illustrations by Robert Griesen.

Assorted material and figures by Marcia L. Tate were originally included in Tate, M. L. (2003). *Worksheets don't grow dendrites: 20 instructional strategies that engage the brain.* Thousand Oaks, CA: Corwin Press.

For information:

Corwin Press
A Sage Publications Company
2455 Teller Road
Thousand Oaks, California 91320
www.corwinpress.com

Sage Publications Ltd.
1 Oliver's Yard
55 City Road
London EC1Y 1SP
United Kingdom

Sage Publications India Pvt. Ltd.
B-42, Panchsheel Enclave
Post Box 4109
New Delhi 110 017 India

Printed in the United States of America

Library of Congress Cataloging-in-Publication Data

Tate, Marcia L.
Reading and language arts worksheets don't grow dendrites: 20 literacy strategies that engage the brain / Marcia L. Tate.
       p. cm.
Includes bibliographical references and index.
    ISBN 978-1-4129-1509-0 (cloth)—ISBN 978-1-4129-1510-6 (pbk.)
1. Language arts. 2. English language—Study and teaching—Activity programs. I. Title.
LB1576.T28 2005
428.' 0071'2—dc22

                                                      2005000623

This book is printed on acid-free paper.

            08   09   10   9 8 7 6 5

Acquisitions Editor:	Rachel Livsey
Editorial Assistant:	Phyllis Cappello
Production Editor:	Melanie Birdsall
Copy Editor:	Elizabeth Budd
Typesetter:	C&M Digitals (P) Ltd.
Proofreader:	Mary Meagher
Indexer:	Michael Ferreira
Cover Designer:	Tracy E. Miller
Graphic Designer:	Lisa Miller

Contents

Introduction

Allow me to tell you a story about Livingston Elementary School. Today is Visitors' Day, when families, friends, and other educators can drop by the classrooms to see what takes place. Imagine a fourth-grade classroom. The teacher is Mrs. Riley, who is required to teach reading and language arts during the first block of the day. She has had little training in this domain and begrudgingly accepted the responsibility because teaching reading comes with the position. Mrs. Riley doesn't love to teach; the way she sees it, at least as a teacher, she'll have her summers free.

Before visitors even enter the classroom, they can hear Mrs. Riley screaming at two students who are talking without permission. When the visitors arrive, Mrs. Riley is not happy to see them and begins to make excuses as to why her lesson plans are not available for review. The lack of visuals on the walls is immediately evident—no student work is displayed, no vocabulary words are posted. Her visitors take seats in the back of the room and begin to observe the lack of activity. They look over the shoulders of several students in the back row and surmise that the students are supposed to be completing vocabulary worksheets on which they circle the most appropriate word for a given sentence. This is one of about 15 worksheets they are to complete. When students finish one, they are instructed to continue to the next one.

Meanwhile, Mrs. Riley takes a seat at her desk and begins to write. It seems as if she is grading papers. She glances up occasionally to see what her visitors are doing (they sense that she feels they are invading her territory) or to reprimand a variety of students for talking when she has demanded absolute silence.

It would seem that this worksheet activity could only last so long and that soon the students will be involved in the authentic task of reading, but this doesn't happen. Thirty minutes later, the majority of students are still at various points in their private worksheet stacks. Some have given up and laid their heads on their desks. Others are obviously angry because they have been told to stay after school, the consequence for not being quiet when instructed to do so. Because there are no lesson plans, it's impossible to know what else will happen within this 90-minute period.

Let's proceed to the classroom of Mr. Benson, a fifth-grade teacher. Because fifth grade is not departmentalized, Mr. Benson must not only teach reading and language arts but all other content areas as well. When his visitors enter the room, Mr. Benson does not notice because he is actively engaged with his students. Discovering the visitors' arrivals, he

warmly greets them and offers places to sit. He then proceeds back to a table where he is conducting a guided-reading group of six students.

What a difference between this class and Mrs. Riley's! The walls are replete with visuals that obviously support classroom instruction. One wall displays content-area vocabulary words arranged alphabetically in clusters. Student work adorns a bulletin board on the back wall. All students are actively engaged. Visitors to the class immediately notice several students sitting on a rug, independently reading books they have selected from the classroom library. Three pairs of students are doing partner reading where they can elect to read a paragraph or a page aloud or pass their turn. They have been taught to read only loud enough for their partner to hear so that they don't disturb other students, who are writing at their desks. They are all writing in journals, composing their own step-by-step explanation for the process of long division. Three students are seated at the computer, surveying the Internet for information related to an upcoming social studies project.

After about 15 minutes, Mr. Benson engages all students in a role play in which they take turns acting out their content-area vocabulary words. The room is filled with laughter as students take turns selecting a given word and trying to get the class to guess the word as they pantomime it. The lesson plan describes a variety of whole-class and small-group activities that have students reading, writing, listening, and talking. This is a classroom the visitors are reluctant to leave.

These are two classrooms in the same school but distinctively different from one another. In Mrs. Riley's classroom, students are engaging in the artificial act of completing countless worksheets, in the hopes that this activity will make them better learners. In Mr. Benson's classroom, authentic tasks ensure that students not only develop the ability to read, but a love of reading as well. After all, students who do not choose to read are no better off than those who do not know how.

THE REAL ACT OF READING ■

I don't remember learning to read. It seems to me that I was born reading because I don't recall a time when I couldn't read. I was fortunate to have been born into a family that valued education and the love of books. I was surrounded by books, and from an early age relatives read aloud to me. My family read and reread nursery rhymes and fairytales until I memorized every line. Eventually, I began to read them for myself. One of my favorite books was *Millions of Cats.* I don't know why I loved that book as a child because I grew up around dogs, not cats, but I fondly remember that as one of the many books I treasured.

In the 21st century, there is good news and bad news. The good news is that there are students who are just as fortunate as I was. They have parents or guardians who talk with them, who read aloud to them, who surround them with good books, and who offer them real-world experiences that appear to translate into literacy. The bad news is there are also those students who, prior to school attendance, have never been talked with, who are not allowed to talk themselves, and who have never been read fairytales, nursery rhymes, or anything else.

Here is better news. Despite the lack of early literate experiences, what if students could enjoy the love of reading while mastering curricular objectives and meeting or exceeding national standards? What if classroom management concerns could all but disappear because students would be motivated and actively engaged in reading and language arts activities? What if all of this could be accomplished with little additional expenditure? If all of the aforementioned were capable of being achieved, would you be interested? If so, have I got an answer for you! Continue reading.

If the single most influential factor in student achievement is the teacher (Sanders & Rivers, 1996), then effective, teacher-directed methodology is essential. Learning style theorists (Gardner, 1983; McCarthy, 1990; Sternberg & Grigorenko, 2000) and researchers (Hannaford, 1995; Diamond & Hopson, 1998) are telling us that there may just be instructional methodologies that, by their very nature, can accomplish all of the aforementioned objectives. These strategies appear to take advantage of the way brains learn best and are mentioned repeatedly in the current literature. There are twenty such strategies so important that by the time a teacher has used them, that teacher has addressed eight of Howard Gardner's multiple intelligences and each of the four major learning modalities—visual, auditory, kinesthetic, and tactile (see Figure 1).

Two books have already been dedicated to the integration of these strategies into professional practice: the bestseller *Worksheets Don't Grow Dendrites: 20 Instructional Strategies That Engage the Brain* and the adult learning text *"Sit & Get" Won't Grow Dendrites: 20 Professional Learning Strategies That Engage the Adult Brain*. This text is dedicated to the application of these 20 strategies toward the way students learn to read and read to learn. Whether you are teaching prekindergarten or SAT Prep, Grade 2 or Grade 12, you would be wise to avail yourself of the strategies, which form the basis of the more than 300 reading and language arts activities contained in this book.

■ RESEARCH RATIONALES

Although some reading and language arts chapters are obviously more appropriate for initial reading instruction in the lower grades (such as phonemic awareness or phonics), the majority of activities contained in the chapters are either appropriate for a variety of grade levels and content areas or they can be adapted and used across the curriculum. For example, the vocabulary instruction activities can be applied to reading vocabulary or used to teach vocabulary in other content areas.

What evidence exists that these brain-compatible strategies also work specifically for delivering reading and language arts instruction? The following rationales suggest that there may be a strong correlation between best practices in this field and the strategies that are delineated in the chapters that follow. The strategies are highlighted in bold for emphasis.

Reading and Language Arts Skills and Abilities Are Best Acquired When Students Are Actively Engaged in Learning (Blachowicz & Fisher, 2002; National Reading Panel, 2000)

There is an ancient Chinese proverb that states the following:

Tell me, I forget.

Show me, I remember.

Involve me, I understand.

Brain-Compatible Reading and Language Arts Strategies	Multiple Intelligences	VAKT
1. Brainstorming and Discussion	Verbal-linguistic	Auditory
2. Drawing and Artwork	Spatial	Kinesthetic-tactile
3. Field Trips	Naturalist	Kinesthetic-tactile
4. Games	Interpersonal	Kinesthetic-tactile
5. Graphic Organizers, Semantic Maps, and Word Webs	Logical-mathematical, Spatial	Visual-tactile
6. Humor	Verbal-linguistic	Auditory
7. Manipulatives	Logical-mathematical	Tactile
8. Metaphors, Analogies, and Similes	Spatial	Visual-auditory
9. Mnemonic Devices	Musical-rhythmic	Visual-auditory
10. Movement	Bodily-kinesthetic	Kinesthetic
11. Music, Rhythm, Rhyme, and Rap	Musical-rhythmic	Auditory
12. Project-Based and Problem-Based Instruction	Logical-mathematical	Visual-tactile
13. Reciprocal Teaching and Cooperative Learning	Verbal-linguistic	Auditory
14. Role Plays, Drama, Pantomimes, and Charades	Bodily-kinesthetic	Kinesthetic
15. Storytelling	Verbal-linguistic	Auditory
16. Technology	Spatial	Visual-tactile
17. Visualization and Guided Imagery	Spatial	Visual
18. Visuals	Spatial	Visual
19. Work Study and Apprenticeships	Interpersonal	Kinesthetic
20. Writing and Journals	Intrapersonal	Visual-tactile

Figure 1   Comparison of Brain-Compatible Reading and Language Arts Strategies to Learning Theory

This timeless saying insinuates that unless students are involved and actively engaged in learning, true learning rarely occurs. By the time a teacher has used all 20 of the brain-compatible strategies delineated here, students have been told, shown, and involved. This includes the delivery of all facets of reading instruction. For example, the Partnership for Reading (2001) relates that the more students are actively engaged with vocabulary over an extended period of time, the more likely they are to learn the words. Blachowicz and Fisher (2002) and Towell (1998) concur. They state that effective vocabulary instruction develops students who are active, who personalize the learning, and who use multiple sources of information to make meaning.

The same is true for comprehension. The National Reading Panel (2000) describes text comprehension as purposeful and active. The techniques and activities a teacher uses to teach reading should be relevant, motivating, and engaging. Many of the activities in this book involve the use of more than one strategy, but an attempt has been made to categorize them according to the predominant strategy used.

Following are the 20 strategies and related research in support of their use for teaching students' reading and language arts skills.

---

20 Brain-Compatible Strategies

1. Brainstorming and Discussion

2. Drawing and Artwork

3. Field Trips

4. Games

5. Graphic Organizers, Semantic Maps, and Word Webs

6. Humor

7. Manipulatives

8. Metaphors, Analogies, and Similes

9. Mnemonic Devices

10. Movement

11. Music, Rhythm, Rhyme, and Rap

12. Project-Based and Problem-Based Instruction

13. Reciprocal Teaching and Cooperative Learning

14. Role Plays, Drama, Pantomimes, and Charades

15. Storytelling

16. Technology

17. Visualization and Guided Imagery

18. Visuals

19. Work Study and Apprenticeships

20. Writing and Journals

Students Learn 90% of What They Talk About or Discuss With Someone Else as They Complete an Assignment (Dale, 1969; Society for Developmental Education, 1995; Sousa, 1995)

Even as far back as 35 years ago, researchers knew that the best way to ensure a student understood a concept was for that student to teach the concept to another student. In fact, until you begin to explain a concept to someone else, you really don't know whether you understand it. Many of the activities in this book afford students opportunities to use **reciprocal teaching** or **brainstorm** and **discuss** so that during whole-class or small-group discussion they can use higher-level thinking skills, increase comprehension, and make the learning their own.

Improvements in Thinking in Art Precede Improvements in Thinking in Other Curricular Areas (Dewey, 1938)

How often have I observed in classrooms only to find students, particularly male ones, doodling or **drawing** pictures that are in no way related to the content being taught. Although students are often reprimanded for this behavior, that talent can be utilized to teach reading. Having students illustrate their vocabulary words or design a book jacket that shows their understanding of the main idea of a story are brain-compatible ways to use the strategy of drawing or artwork in teaching reading and language arts. There are even studies that show significantly higher reading scores for students who took arts-enriched classes as opposed to those who did not (College Board, 2000; Gardiner, 1996).

In addition, the use of **manipulatives** to enhance reading and language arts instruction is supported by the strong interrelatedness between the hands and the brain. So related are they, in fact, that there is no one theory to explain it (Jensen, 2001). We do know that having students sort vocabulary cards, write in a salt or sand tray, or manipulate magnetic letters facilitate learning.

When Students Go to Places in the Real World, Solve Real-World Problems, or Complete Real-World Projects, Their Brains Are Placed Closer to the Reason for Which They Were Created—That is, for Survival (Westwater & Wolfe, 2000)

It is this research that provides the rationale for why **field trips**, **project-based instruction**, **problem-based instruction**, and **work study** are such meaningful strategies for the brain. When students read related literature before a field trip or locate pertinent information that will assist them in completing a project or solving a problem, learning increases. In this text, activities are described that will engage students in authentic reading and language arts tasks in which English skills are integrated in real-world contexts rather than taught separately on a worksheet or in an English textbook.

When Students Have Fun, Learning Is Facilitated (Burgess, 2000; Pert, 1997)

Both **humor** and **games,** two of the most motivating strategies, are naturals for teaching reading and language arts. Having students walk a path as they name each high-frequency word written on the footprints or pronounce each sight word as they move markers along a path in an attempt to beat a partner to the finish line are both great ways to ensure mastery through repetition. Towell (1998) relates that vocabulary instruction should be as much fun as it possibly can be. She describes how riddles can be used to introduce new vocabulary words for stories and can be a component of thematic units in an integrated curriculum. After all, the humor derived from riddles and jokes not only strengthens memory but the immune system as well, rendering an individual less susceptible to disease and illness (Cardoso, 2000; Pert, 1997).

Graphic Organizers Are Very Effective Strategies for Both the Left and Right Hemispheres of the Brain (Buzan & Buzan, 1994)

The majority of strategies on the list of 20 are brain-compatible because they can be used to teach to both hemispheres of the brain. This fact is important because both left and right hemispheres talk to one another over the corpus callosum, the structure that connects them. No strategy is better designed for this purpose than the **graphic organizer.** Semantic, concept, or thinking maps as well as word webs are great ways to show connections between and among content. Rupley et al. (1999) relates that graphic organizers, such as semantic maps, semantic feature analysis, and webbing, are effective strategies for actively processing vocabulary.

Activities contained in this book enable students to design an antonym or synonym word web. Graphic organizers are provided that help to teach and reinforce the skills of main idea and details, sequence of events, character traits and motives, and cause and effect. Students are also taught to design their own graphic organizers to help them in comprehending both narrative and expository texts.

Metaphors Enable Students to Make Connections Among Texts (Caine & Caine, 1994; Gregory & Chapman, 2002)

One of the best ways for ensuring that the brain retains new information is to connect it to information that the brain already knows. People who think in **metaphors, analogies, and similes** think at higher levels. The

Miller's Analogy Test is even used to determine a person's ability to be successful at the graduate level. Gregory and Chapman (2002) encourage the use of metaphors because this strategy broadens students' thinking and makes it more likely that comprehension will be extended and retained in the future.

Metaphorical connections are made throughout this book. For example, when teaching the concept of main idea, an effective technique is to compare it to the top of a table. Just like a table top needs support, so does a main idea. Just as the legs of the table support the top, so do the details support the main idea of the text. When I was a reading specialist, students in my reading classes always understood this simile, and it helped them understand the concept.

Mnemonic Devices, or Brain Shortcuts, Can Assist Students in Learning Two to Three Times More Than Students Who Learn Through Other Methods (Markowitz & Jensen, 1999)

DEAR (Drop Everything and Read) Time

i before e except after c

When two vowels go walking, the first one does the talking.

Teachers have always had ways to engage student brains in the memory of rules and principles for learning to read. Some of these ways involve the use of **mnemonic devices,** acronyms and acrostics for helping the brain remember key terms. In fact, the word *mnemonic* originates from the Greek word *mnema,* which is defined as memory. Acronyms are words made from the initial letter of each word in the phrase that is to be remembered. For example, the word HOMES actually represents each of the Great Lakes: *Huron, Ontario, Michigan, Erie,* and *Superior.* Acrostics are sentences in which the first letter of the concept to be memorized is reflected in the first letter of each word in a corresponding sentence. For example, *Every Good Boy Does Fine* actually represents the line notes on the treble clef, EGBDF.

When Both Body and Brain Are Actively Engaged in Learning, Information Is Placed in Procedural Memory, One of the Strongest Memory Systems (Jensen, 2000; Sprenger, 1999)

I love using **movement** and **role play** to teach students reading and language arts skills. Remember the Chinese proverb: *Involve me, I understand.* The most powerful aid to understanding is active involvement. With little effort, students can learn to act out vocabulary words, perform a reader's theater, form a simple or complex sentence, or move into a cause-and-effect chain.

Why does memory improve when the body gets involved in the learning? Because the body places information in one of the strongest memory systems in the brain—procedural memory. Skills one learns when the body is engaged, such as driving a car or riding a bike, are long remembered. It stands to reason then that when students are standing, walking, clapping, or jumping as they review or master content, their procedural memories are strengthened (Sprenger, 1999).

Music Can Be a Powerful Motivator for Acquiring Reading and Language Arts Skills (Towell, 1998)

Although **music** can change the state, or mood, of the brain and even help to develop that spatial part of the brain that is involved when it is problem solving or thinking critically, music's major claim to fame is its ability to help you remember. Whatever the brain is able to put to music, it tends to recall long term.

Towell (1998) recommends music as a motivator for learning vocabulary words or developing phonemic awareness. Songs and chants are ideal for developing a young child's recognition of the structures of sounds in language. You will find activities in this book that teach reading and language arts through song lyrics or that use rhymes, chants, and raps to teach sight words, recall vocabulary definitions, demonstrate comprehension, or acquire language arts skills.

When Students Are Listening to Stories, They Are Utilizing the Frontal Lobes of the Brain to Follow the Plot (Storm, 1999)

Whether a speaker, minister, or teacher, anyone who talks to either children or adults would do well to use the age-old strategy of **storytelling**. When a good story is told, everyone listens. It would stand to reason that a book of effective reading and language arts strategies would be replete with the use of stories. An expanded use for stories is as a vehicle for teaching skills and strategies. Following the reading of a story for enjoyment, students could revisit the literature to do any of the following: locate a designated high-frequency or vocabulary word, find the main idea or sequence of events, select a complex sentence contained within the context, or design a graphic organizer that depicts the main idea and details. Stories connect information together for the brain. They have beginnings, middles, and endings. They are sequential in nature and offer wonderful tools for holistic teaching.

Computer Technology Can Be Used to Teach Vocabulary Effectively (National Reading Panel, 2000)

101 Misused Words and How to Use Them Correctly by Learning Seed and *Survival Word Play* by J. Weston Welch are just two of the programs that incorporate **technology** as a means of introducing, teaching, or reviewing reading or language arts skills. Having students research Web sites or create a PowerPoint presentation to symbolize what they have learned in a social studies or science chapter is most beneficial. Computers have even been found to be effective in teaching and reinforcing phonemic awareness in young children. As a brain strategy, it certainly has its place. However, if the task that a student performs on the computer resembles a similar task on a drill and kill worksheet, then it becomes just another way to simulate an ineffective practice.

More Information Goes Into the Brain Visually Than Through Any Other Modality (Miller, 2002)

There are probably more learners sitting in classrooms today who are strong in the visual modality than learners of any other type. Therefore, anything a teacher can do to facilitate understanding of text through the use of **visuals** is greatly appreciated by today's brains. This may mean bringing in a picture or likeness of a vocabulary word to be taught so that students have a visual image of the unfamiliar term. It may mean teaching students to use picture cues as they attempt to read and comprehend text. It may mean surveying a content-area text book before reading a chapter or unit of study and looking at charts, graphs, picture captions, and diagrams to ascertain some understanding of what will be read.

Because 95% of what the brain takes does not come in from direct instruction but as unconscious learning, it stands to reason that even the eight parts of speech displayed on the classroom door or the vocabulary categorized on the word wall all contribute to the brain's storehouse of knowledge and information.

Another of the 20 strategies is **visualization.** Coaches find this technique helpful when they ask their athletes to visualize themselves scoring the touchdown or hitting the homerun before the start of the game. The same technique works for students. Proficient readers use all five senses to form mental images which help them recall significant details in the text, draw conclusions, and create interpretations of the text (Miller, 2002).

Both Long- and Short-Term Memory Are Improved Through Writing (Hadwin, Kirby, & Woodhouse, 1999)

It is amazing that the things one writes down are more easily remembered. It even appears that a person is more likely to accomplish stated goals if they are written down. **Writing** is such a crucial part of a language arts program that writing activities are not only part of each chapter in this book, a whole chapter is devoted to it in the Language Arts section. It is a skill that can and should be used in every content area across the curriculum. When teachers provide students with opportunities to take notes in short chunks of information, retention is facilitated.

ORGANIZATIONAL STRUCTURE ■

This book is divided into two major sections: Reading and Language Arts. The Reading chapters comprise half of the book and are organized around the major categories delineated in the groundbreaking *Report of the*

National Reading Panel: An Evidence-based Assessment of the Scientific Research Literature on Reading and Its Implications for Reading Instruction (National Reading Panel, 2000). This report, commissioned by congress, represents the panel's comprehensive conclusions regarding the most pertinent research on effective reading instruction in schools.

Reading is crucial to one's ability to be successful in every other content area and should in no way be separated from language arts. Therefore, the second half of this book is organized according to the following major themes of the 12 *Standards for the English Language Arts,* developed jointly by the International Reading Association (IRA) and the National Council of Teachers of English (NCTE). The 12 Standards are as follows:

1. Students read from a wide range of print and nonprint texts to build an understanding of texts, of themselves, and of the cultures of the United States and the world to acquire new information; to respond to the needs and demands of society and the workplace; and for personal fulfillment. Among these texts are fiction, nonfiction, classic, and contemporary works.

2. Students read a wide range of literature from many periods in many genres to build an understanding of the many dimensions (e.g., philosophical, ethical, aesthetic) of human experience.

3. Students apply a wide range of strategies to comprehend, interpret, evaluate, and appreciate texts. They draw on their prior experience, their interactions with other readers and writers, their knowledge of word meaning and of other texts, their word identification strategies, and their understanding of textual features (e.g., sound-letter correspondence, sentence structure, context, graphics).

4. Students adjust their use of spoken, written, and visual language (e.g., conventions, style, vocabulary) to communicate effectively with a variety of audiences and for different purposes.

5. Students employ a wide range of strategies as they write and use different writing process elements appropriately to communicate with different audiences and for different purposes.

6. Students apply knowledge of language structure, language conventions (e.g., spelling and punctuation), media techniques, figurative language, and genre to create, critique, and discuss print and nonprint texts.

7. Students conduct research on issues and interests by generating ideas and questions, and by posing problems. They gather, evaluate, and synthesize data from a variety of sources (e.g., print and nonprint texts, artifacts, people) to communicate their discoveries in ways that suit their purpose and audience.

8. Students use a variety of technological and informational resources (e.g., libraries, databases, computer networks, video) to gather and synthesize information and to create and communicate knowledge.

9. Students develop an understanding of respect for diversity in language use, patterns, and dialects across cultures, ethnic groups, geographic regions, and social roles.

10. Students whose first language is not English make use of their language to develop competency in the English language arts and to develop understanding of content across the curriculum.

11. Students participate as knowledgeable, reflective, creative, and critical members of a variety of literacy communities.

12. Students use spoken, written, and visual language to accomplish their own purposes (e.g., for learning, enjoyment, persuasion, and the exchange of information).

Each chapter provides an explanation of the reading or language arts category, summarizes the relevant research in the designated area, and provides classroom activities that teachers can use to integrate the 20 strategies into instruction. In most cases, more than one of the 20 strategies will be inherent in a given activity; however, each activity is categorized under the strategy that is most emphasized during its implementation. At the end of each chapter, an opportunity is provided for the reader to reflect on the activities presented and determine which ones would be most appropriate for a particular group of students. This would also be a good time to decide which activities might be adapted for implementation across the curriculum.

The last section of this book outlines five pertinent questions every teacher of reading and language arts should ask when planning a lesson. These questions will help to ensure that every lesson utilizes the strategies and is planned in the most brain-compatible way possible.

Watch what happens to your reading and language arts classroom when student brains are actively engaged in meaningful instruction. If you could maximize reading achievement for all students—gifted, regular education, and special education alike—while enjoying teaching and learning and all at little additional expenditure, failing to do so should be termed professional malpractice. In fact, the slogan from Nike advertisements is applicable here—*Just Do It!*

Acknowledgments

More than 30 years ago, I completed a program of study that certified me as a reading specialist. I am happy to say that over many years, I have taught large numbers of students to read. Even before I knew about brain research, I knew that at least 80% of my job as a teacher of reading was to give my students the confidence to believe that they could learn to read. The other 20% required teaching them to read. Once they had the confidence, however, teaching them was easy. Helping them to gain confidence was much more difficult because many of the students I taught were five, six, or even seven years below grade level in their reading ability.

This book is dedicated to teachers everywhere who give students the confidence to believe that they can read well. The 20 brain-compatible strategies and more than 300 activities contained in this book are designed to assist these teachers in their noble efforts. May you and your students enjoy teaching and learning because with that enjoyment comes increased academic achievement and decreased classroom management concerns.

I thank my mother, Eurica, and my father, Alvin, for the gift of literacy. Thank you for surrounding me with books and the importance of reading. Because all parents are their children's best and first teachers, I am grateful that you did your job and did it well. I, too, have tried to do equally as well for my own children—Jennifer, Jessica, and Chris.

I deeply appreciate the continued support of those closest to me, especially my husband, Tyrone, who enables me to do what I do to the best of my ability. Our gratitude goes to the associates who work tirelessly with our company, Developing Minds, Inc., and help us spread the word that all students truly can learn when they are taught in ways that are brain compatible!

The contributions of the following reviewers are gratefully acknowledged:

Catherine Duffy
English Chairperson
Three Village Central School District
Setauket, NY

Carrice Cummins
Associate Professor
Louisiana Tech University
Ruston, LA

Debra Puente
Reading/Language Arts Coordinator/Administrator
Monterey County Office of Education
Salinas, CA

About the Author

**Marcia L. Tate, EdD,** is the former Executive Director of Professional Development for the DeKalb County School System, Decatur, Georgia. During her 30-year career with the district, she has been a classroom teacher, reading specialist, language arts coordinator, and staff development executive director. Marcia received the Distinguished Staff Developer Award for the state of Georgia, and her department was chosen to receive the 2002 Exemplary Program Award for the state.

Marcia is also an educational consultant and CEO of Developing Minds, Inc. She has presented to more than 100,000 administrators, teachers, parents, and business and community leaders around the world. She is a member of the National Speaker's Bureau for Corwin Press and has presented at numerous state, national, and international conferences. Her first book, *Worksheets Don't Grow Dendrites: 20 Instructional Strategies That Engage the Brain,* is a bestseller. Her second book, *"Sit & Get" Won't Grow Dendrites: 20 Professional Learning Strategies That Engage the Adult Brain,* provides brain-compatible recommendations for engaging adults in quality professional learning. Marcia's workshops receive rave reviews because she uses the 20 brain-compatible strategies outlined in both books to engage her audience. In 2002, Marcia was featured in a national teleconference, Brain-Friendly Reading, along with Carolyn Chapman.

Marcia holds a bachelor's degree in psychology and elementary education from Spelman College, a master of arts degree in remedial reading from the University of Michigan, an educational specialist degree from Georgia State University, and a doctorate in educational leadership from Clark Atlanta University. Spelman College awarded her the Apple Award for excellence in the field of education.

Marcia is married to Tyrone Tate and is the proud mother of three children: Jennifer, also a teacher; Jessica, a recent college graduate; and Christopher, a high school student. Marcia can be contacted by calling her company, Developing Minds, Inc., at (770) 918-5039 or by e-mail: marciata @bellsouth.net. Visit her Web site at www.developingmindsinc.com.

PART I
Reading Strategies

1

Phonemic Awareness

Phonemic awareness should be playful, engaging, interactive, and social.

—Yopp, 1995

A phoneme is defined as the smallest unit comprising spoken language. In the English language, there appear to be almost 50 phonemes. In fact, before excited parents hear their baby say "mama" and "dada," that baby has already said 47 other phonemes (P. Leach, 1995, as cited on *Prime Time Live*, ABC News). Unfortunately, none of the other phonemes the baby said gain quite the attention of those two magic words that all parents love to hear.

Alphabet recognition and phonemic awareness—*the ability of the student to focus on or manipulate phonemes in spoken words*—have been identified by correlational studies as the two best predictors of how well students will acquire reading skills during their first two years of school (National Reading Panel, 2000). Fluency in reading begins when students are capable of hearing and recognizing individual sounds in speech, when students know that spoken words and syllables are composed of a series of spoken sounds, and when they realize that if one letter is changed in a word, it can completely change the meaning (Teele, 2004).

Instruction in this area should move from the easier skills of phoneme identity and isolation to the more difficult skills of categorization, blending, segmentation, and deletion. A brief description of each skill follows. Phoneme isolation asks students to recognize the individual sounds in one word; for example, *What is the first sound that you hear in the word fast (/f/)?* Phoneme identity requires that students identify the sounds that are alike at the beginning, middle, or ending of two or more words. An example would be, *What sound is the same in the words* mat, mix, *and* mud? Phrases that exemplify alliteration are helpful in teaching phoneme identification; for example, *Sally sells seashells down by the seashore* or *The nice neat night nurse needs new nylons.*

Phoneme categorization or so-called oddity tasks require a student to determine whether two or more spoken words are the same or different or to identify the odd word in a series of three or more words. Examples of this skill are as follows: *Which word does not belong: tan, van, house, man? Which word does not begin with the same sound as the other words: cat, boy, car, can?* More difficult tasks include the following: *Which of the following words do not end with the same sound: run, can, sat? Which of the following words do not have the same middle sound: pig, sit, lap?*

Phoneme blending requires that students listen for individual sounds and blend them into a known word; for example, *What is the following word: /s/ /p/ /u/ /l/ (spool)?* Segmentation of phonemes occurs when students are asked to count or mark the individual sounds in a word: *How many different phonemes do you hear in the word drip?*

One of the most difficult skills in this area is phonemic deletion or having students recognize what word parts remain when a specific phoneme is removed. An example would be, *What would bread be without the /ead/?*

Although activities will be provided for each of the aforementioned types of phonemic manipulation, research has shown that instruction focusing on only one or two types, such as blending or segmentation, is far superior to that which focuses on several types (National Reading Panel, 2000; Partnership for Reading, 2001). This may be due to a number of factors, including the confusion caused when too many types are taught at one time, the limited amount of time the teacher can spend on any one type, or the student's inability to master the easier manipulations before proceeding to the more difficult ones. The activities that follow will be instrumental in incorporating brain-compatible strategies to help students acquire phonemic awareness skills. Students do not realize that while they are playing games, working with a partner, or singing a song, they are actually laying the foundation for the acquisition of reading skills.

RELEVANT RESEARCH

When the 26 letters of the alphabet are introduced prior to the sounds, 12 of the phonemes are not included (Wolfe & Nevills, 2004).

Poetry strengthens students' oral and written language abilities, expands their knowledge of content, and adds to their knowledge of social skills (Pinnell & Fountas, 2004).

Hearing syllables in words has been considered the bridge between children's ability to hear a phoneme and their ability to hear a word. This skill has been identified as a predictor of future reading ability (Wolfe & Nevills, 2004).

Phonemic awareness activities should be playful and interactive and are best taught within the context of authentic reading and writing and not in isolation (Anderson, 2004; Wolfe & Nevills, 2004).

Students acquire phonemic awareness best when they are taught using a wide variety of teaching methods that match their learning styles (Teele, 2004).

When the brain is involved in phonemic awareness, oral language neural pathways are reshaped and will be used later for reading (Wolfe & Nevills, 2004).

Instruction in phonemic awareness can help improve the reading and spelling abilities of all students including beginning readers and older, less capable ones (Partnership for Reading, 2001).

A well-executed phonemic awareness program should take no more than 20 hours of class time throughout an entire school year with instruction differentiated based on need (Partnership for Reading, 2001).

A number of reading experts attribute reading difficulties in children and adults to a lack of phonemic awareness (Adams, Foorman, Lundberg, & Beeler, 1998; Lyon and Fletcher, 2001).

It is better to concentrate on only one or two types of phonemic instruction rather than instructing in several types (Partnership for Reading, 2001).

The connection between phonemic awareness and real reading should be clear and explicit to the student (Partnership for Reading, 2001).

Instructing students in the manipulation of phonemes in words yielded highly effective results whether students were reading words, pseudo-words, or comprehending (National Reading Panel, 2000).

When phoneme manipulation was taught with the accompanying letters, children acquired phonemic awareness better than when it was taught without letters (National Reading Panel, 2000).

Children taught to manipulate phonemes with accompanying letters were better spellers than those who were taught phonemes only through speech (National Reading Panel, 2000).

When the brain's angular gyrus is damaged, reading and writing are not possible because it is within this structure that letters are translated into sounds or phonemes (Carter, 1998).

Phonemic awareness should be playful, engaging, interactive, and social (Yopp, 1995).

An effective approach for developing phonemic awareness along with word identification and spelling is the use of word boxes (Clay, 1993; Yopp, 1995).

Teachers should be encouraged to stimulate students linguistically with strategies such as storytelling, word games, rhymes, and riddles in order to facilitate phonemic awareness (Mattingly, 1984).

STRATEGIC ACTIVITIES

Objective: Recognize individual sounds in words (phoneme isolation)

Brainstorming and Discussion

• Read the following list of words aloud. Have students discuss the first sound they hear in each word: 1. bear /b/ 2. fast /f/ 3. hat /h/ 4. man /m/ 5. bat /b/

• Read a sample alphabet book aloud to students for enjoyment. Have students work together to make a class alphabet book. Have them brainstorm words with the same beginning phoneme as the chosen letter of the alphabet. For example, for the letter D, the alphabet book could read *David does daily dances.* For the letter P, the alphabet book could read *Penny puts pebbles in piles.*

Manipulatives

• Stuff small plastic bags with objects and the same number of interlocking cubes as there are phonemes in the object. For example, in one bag could be a nut and three cubes that are connected for the three sounds in the word nut. Distribute the bags to students in the class. Each student opens the bag, and pulls out the object and the cubes. The student names the object and then says the sounds in the object as she or he breaks apart the cube (Yopp & Yopp, 2000).

Movement

• Have students say the phoneme that represents the first sound in a given name and then stand if their name begins with that same phoneme. For example, say the following to students: *Tell me the first sound you hear in the name James. If your name also begins with that same sound, please stand.*

• Read the story *A, My Name is Alice* by Jane Bayer (1984) for enjoyment. Following several readings, have students jump rope as they say several selected rhymes in the book. Following this activity, have them name the first sound they hear in the jump rope rhymes. For example, students tell the beginning sound they hear in the following rhyme:

A, My name is Alice, and my husband's name is Alex.

We come from Alaska, and we sell ants.

Alice is an aardvark, and Alex is an anteater.

Students work together to write other verses to the rhyme using the names of students in the class.

- Students work in pairs or trios to walk around the room finding objects that begin with the same sound as a given picture. For example, a trio is given the picture of a dog. The three students then work together to find objects in the room that begin with the /d/ sound. Objects located could include a desk, some dust, or a door.

Music, Rhythm, Rhyme, and Rap

- Use music to teach phonemes by having students sing several of their favorite songs. Following many repetitions, select key words from the lyrics and have students name the first sound they hear in each word. For example, in the song "Twinkle, Twinkle Little Star," students could name the first sound they hear in the following words: how, above, like, diamond.

- Rhyme is effective for teaching ending phonemes. Have students identify the ending phonemes in some favorite nursery rhymes such as *Little Miss Muffet sat on a tuffet, The itsy bitsy spider crawled up the water spout,* or *Jack and Jill went up the hill.*

- Have students rewrite a favorite nursery rhyme to change the ending phonemes. For example, *Mary, Mary, quite contrary, how does your garden grow?* could be rewritten as *Johnny, Johnny, just as funny, why do you tease us so?*

Storytelling

- Read aloud one of the favorite stories of the class. Following several readings simply for enjoyment of the literature, select key words from the story and have students name the first sound they hear in each word.

Objective: Recognize the common sound in different words (phoneme identity)

Drawing and Artwork

- Select nouns that have the same beginning, middle, or ending phoneme. Each student draws a picture of one of the nouns selected. Have one student come to the front of the room and bring his or her drawing. Ask the student to tell the sound at the beginning, middle, or ending of the noun that they drew. Any student who drew a word with the same beginning, middle, or ending sound also comes to the front of the room. For example, say to students, *Would the student who drew the picture of a word that begins with the /t/ sound please come to the front of the room?* The student who drew the tiger would come to the front. Then say, *If you drew a word that begins like "tiger," would you come to the front as well?* Students who drew pictures of a table or telephone would also come to the front of the room. Follow the same procedure for the middle and ending phonemes in selected nouns.

Adaptation: Have three or four students come to the front of the room with their drawings. Have students decide whether any of the three words begin or end with the same phonemes.

Movement

• Have students stand if the two words read have the same beginning phoneme and remain seated if the two beginning phonemes are different. Once students become proficient with beginning phonemes, have them listen for and stand if two words have the same ending or middle phoneme.

Storytelling

• Read aloud one of the favorite stories of the class. Following several readings simply for enjoyment of the literature, select key words from the story and show students that these words have the same beginning, middle, or ending phoneme.

Objective: Recognize the word with a different sound in a series of three or more words (phoneme categorization)

Brainstorming and Discussion

• Pronounce a series of three or four words for students. One word in each series should have a different beginning, middle, or ending phoneme from the other words in the series. Students would discuss which word is not the same. For example, in the series *man, sad, bat,* and *pig,* students would identify that *pig* would be the word that does not belong because it is the only word with a different phoneme in the middle.

Drawing and Artwork

• Have students brainstorm and draw three pictures, two with the same beginning, middle, or ending phoneme, and one with a different phoneme from the other two. For example, students could draw pictures of the words *finger, farm, and man.* Students would explain to the class that *finger* and *farm* begin with the same phoneme and *man* does not.

Metaphors, Analogies, and Similes

• Have four students come to the front of the room with three of the four having something in common, such as three boys and one girl or three students without glasses and one student with glasses. Have the remainder of the class guess which student does not belong and tell why.

Movement

• Brainstorm a list of words that have the same beginning, middle, or ending phoneme. Write the words on cards and pass them out randomly to students. Have students move around the room and find other students holding words with the same beginning, middle, or ending phonemes as the words they have. They then stand next to the selected student(s). Pick three students who have words with the same phonemes and one with a word that is not the same. Allow students to determine the different phoneme.

Objective: Combine a sequence of separately spoken words into a recognizable word (phoneme blending)

Manipulatives

• Give each student three phonemes that can be blended together to make a word. For example, one student has the following phoneme cards: /b/, /e/, /d/. Another student has the following cards: /p/, /i/, /g/. Students place their phonemes in an order that will make a word. They then blend them together and pronounce the word for their partner. Students see whether they can combine any of their phonemes and those of their partner in a different order to make another word.

Metaphors, Analogies, and Similes

• Compare the blending of phonemes to the blending or mixing of paint by showing students that when you mix together yellow and red paint, you get the color orange. Similarly, when you mix two sounds together, you get another sound that is a blend of the single sounds. Give students examples of words with blended beginning sounds such as play, bread, grape, and swing.

Role Plays, Drama, Pantomimes, and Charades

• Ask two students to come to the front of the class. Pronounce the word *black.* Explain to students that at the beginning of the word black are two sounds that like each other very much, so they work together. Name one student the /b/ sound and the other student the /l/ sound. Have the two students stand close together to demonstrate that these two sounds blend together. Pronounce the two sounds blended together and have students do the same /bl/. Have other students come to the front of the room and role play the following additional blended phonemes: /pl/ as in play, /cl/ as in clock, and /fl/ as in flower. When students appear to comprehend blends with the letter /l/, use examples of other blended words such as /br/ in bread, /sk/ as in skate, or /tw/ as in twinkle.

Movement

- Each student is given a phoneme that could be combined with another student's phoneme to make a word. For example, one student could be given the phoneme /f/, another the phoneme /u/, and another the phoneme /n/. Play music with a fast pace and have students walk around the room until they find another student with a phoneme they can combine with their own to make a word. When they find that student, they stand together. When the music stops, have the class pronounce all of the words made by the students standing together.

Music, Rhythm, Rhyme, and Rap

- Use music to teach blended phonemes by having students sing several of their favorite songs. Following many repetitions, select key words from the lyrics and have students name the first two sounds they hear in each blended word. Two examples follow. In the song "Twinkle, Twinkle, Little Star," students could name the two sounds they hear in the following words and blend them together: twinkle, star, sky. In the song, "Baa, Baa, Black Sheep, Have You Any Wool?" students could name the two sounds they hear at the beginning of the word *black*.

Writing and Journals

- Teach students how to blend phonemes by doing the following: Pronounce the phonemes /b/, /i/, /g/ for students. Ask students what word you just said. Then say, *Let's write the letters which represent the sounds in* big. *We're going to read the word* big. Provide additional practice by repeating the procedure with the following phonemes: /c/, /a/, /t/ (cat); /b/, /u/, /g/ (bug); /s/, /i/, /p/ (sip).

Objective: Break a word into its separate sounds (phoneme segmentation)

Manipulatives

- Draw a word box, a rectangle that is divided into sections that correspond to the sounds heard in a key word. A picture could be placed above the boxes. Place counters below the divided sections of the rectangle. As the student slowly pronounces each sound in the key word, the student places counters in the respective boxes. For example, give a student a word box divided into three sections. Above the word boxes is a picture of a cat. As the student pronounces the /c/ sound, the student puts a counter in the first box. The student pronounces the /a/ sound and places the second counter in the second divided section of the box, and then as the student pronounces the /t/ sound, a counter is placed in the last section. An example follows:

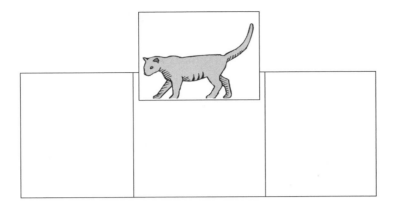

Adaptation: The student can eventually replace the counters with magnetic letters representing the sounds.

Adaptation: The student can spell the word by writing the letters in the sections of the box as the student hears the sounds in the word (Clay, 1993; Joseph, 1999).

Movement

• Students listen to a given word as the teacher pronounces it. Students clap once for each phoneme in the given word as the word is repeated. Begin with words that have two phonemes and expand to three or more.

• Students listen to a given word as the teacher pronounces it. Students stomp their feet once for each phoneme in the given word.

• Students listen to a given word as the teacher pronounces it. Students touch a different body part to represent the order of each phoneme in the word. For example, for the word *sun* students touch their heads as they pronounce the /s/, their waists as they pronounce the /u/, and their feet as they pronounce /n/.

Reciprocal Teaching and Cooperative Learning

• Students count the number of separate phonemes in a word pronounced by the teacher and compare the number with their close partner.

Objective: Recognize the remaining word when a specific phoneme is changed (phoneme deletion, addition, substitution)

Brainstorming and Discussion

• Write a word on the board. Have students discuss the word that remains when one phoneme is deleted. For example, ask students, *What is*

the word swing *without the s?* The students would say *wing.* Provide numerous additional examples.

- Write a word on the board. Have students discuss the word that is formed when another phoneme is added. For example, ask students, *What is the word* late *with the /s/ sound added?* The students would say *slate.* Provide numerous additional examples.

- Write a word on the board. Have students discuss the word that is formed when another phoneme is substituted. For example, say to students, *The word is pat. Change the /t/ to /d/. What is the new word?* Provide numerous additional examples.

Manipulatives

- Give students word cards that contain the phonemes in a given word such as *bus.* Have them place the cards on their desk to spell the word. As you name a phoneme, have them remove it from their desk and pronounce the phonemes that remain. For example, *What is bus without the /b/? us. What is bus without the /s/? bu.*

As students become more proficient, use longer words with more sophisticated phonemes.

Movement

- Have the same number of students come to the front of the room as there are phonemes in a given word. Give each student a card with a letter that represents each phoneme in the given word. Then delete, add, or substitute phonemes by deleting, adding, or substituting students. For example, have three students come to the front of the class. Give each student a letter card that represents the phonemes in *tan.* One student would have the /t/, one student the /a/, and one student the /n/. Have them stand close together, and have the class pronounce the word *tan.* Have the student with the /t/ sit down. Ask students what word would remain? They respond, *an.* Then give another student a word card with the phoneme /s/. Have that student come to the front of the class and stand at the beginning of the word tan to make the word Stan. Have students pronounce the new word. Finally, have the /s/ and the /t/ sit down, and have other students come to the front of the room. Give each of these students initial phonemes to substitute for the /t/ in the word *tan.* One student could come with a /D/, one with an /f/, and one with a /v/. Have students pronounce the new words *Dan, fan,* and *van.*

REFLECTION AND APPLICATION

> ## Which strategies can I use to teach phonemic awareness so that my students' brains are engaged?

Standard/Objective: _____

_____

_____.

Activity: _____

_____

_____.

Standard/Objective: _____

_____

_____.

Activity: _____

_____

_____.

Standard/Objective: _____

_____

_____.

Activity: _____

_____

_____.

Standard/Objective: _____

_____

_____.

Activity: _____

_____

_____.

Standard/Objective: _____

_____

_____.

Activity: _____

_____

_____.

2

Phonics Instruction

Reading = D × C

Reading = Decoding × Comprehension

—Phil Gough, Reading Researcher

When I think of phonics instruction, I think only of two childhood memories: coloring the pictures on countless worksheets and writing the initial, middle, and ending sounds of words represented by those pictures. Isn't it ironic that I was already reading when I was given these tasks? In fact, I did not learn the sounds associated with vowels until I was in graduate school studying to be a reading specialist.

What we know today is that although effective phonics instruction is but one of the building blocks in a complete reading program, it is a foundational building block. It enables the reader to decode rapidly the pronunciation of unknown words so that comprehension is not negatively affected (Wolfe & Nevills, 2004). Systematic phonics instruction, the type of instruction that is most beneficial to the student, identifies a specially selected set of letter–sound relationships structured in a logical order (Partnership for Reading, 2001).

Several systematic and sequential approaches form the basis for phonics instruction. Some phonics programs are actually a combination of several approaches. According to the National Reading Panel (2000), several of the main types are delineated in the paragraphs that follow. Synthetic phonics programs teach the alphabet letters first, how to convert those letters into phonemes or sounds, and then how to blend the isolated sounds into familiar words. Analytic phonics teaches students to analyze the sounds in words only after the words have been identified. Phonics-through-spelling programs instruct students in changing sounds into letters for the purpose of writing words, whereas phonics-in-context programs teach letter-sound associations in concert with the context of the reading selection. Analogy phonics programs assist students in using the parts of the words they do know to identify unfamiliar words. One thing these programs have in common is that they help students understand that alphabet letters, or graphemes, represent the smallest sounds in spoken language, called phonemes. This knowledge allows readers to crack the reading code, which is made more difficult by the inconsistencies and irregularities in the English language. The findings of the National Reading Panel (2000) relating to phonics instruction will be delineated in the Relevant Research section of this chapter.

This chapter does not cover all of the phonics skills but provides strategies for rhyming words, initial and final consonant sounds, consonant blends and digraphs, and vowel sounds. All of these activities can be modified and applied to skills that are not contained in the chapter. That is what the Reflection and Application page enables the reader to do. Refer to Chapter 1, "Phonemic Awareness," for additional activities that teach or reinforce beginning, medial, or ending sounds.

RELEVANT RESEARCH

Phonics instruction is not a reading program in and of itself (Wolfe & Nevills, 2004).

Systematic and explicit phonics, when introduced early, significantly improves kindergarten and first-grade children's word recognition, spelling, and reading comprehension; benefits students from varying socioeconomic levels; and is specifically helpful for students experiencing difficulty learning to read (Partnership for Reading, 2001).

Students must have ample time to practice their knowledge of letter-sound relationships during real reading and writing activities (Partnership for Reading, 2001).

Systematic phonics instruction correlates more positively with students' growth in reading than do alternative programs or no phonics instruction at all (National Reading Panel, 2000).

Various systematic phonics programs all appeared consistently effective and all more effective than programs without phonics instruction (National Reading Panel, 2000).

Systematic phonics instruction can be effective in a variety of delivery methods including tutoring, small-group, and whole-class instruction (National Reading Panel, 2000).

Systematic phonics instruction is most effective when begun in kindergarten or first grade prior to the time when students are taught to read independently (National Reading Panel, 2000).

Systematic phonics instruction is more beneficial than instruction without phonics for preventing reading problems among students at risk for reading failure and in remediating students who already have reading difficulties (National Reading Panel, 2000).

Systematic phonics instruction led to greater achievement in text comprehension than nonphonics instruction in kindergarten and first-grade children. Results were uncertain for students above first grade (National Reading Panel, 2000).

Systematic phonics instruction resulted in increased growth in spelling for kindergarten and first-grade students but not for students above first grade (National Reading Panel, 2000).

Students of all socioeconomic levels can benefit from systematic phonics instruction (National Reading Panel, 2000).

Systematic phonics instruction resulted in students who outperformed peers taught in a number of nonsystematic or nonphonics programs, including whole language programs, basal programs, or whole word programs (National Reading Panel, 2000).

When the techniques a teacher uses to teach phonics are motivating, engaging, and fun, students will be more successful (National Reading Panel, 2000).

The explicit sounds should be taught first, followed by the letter or letters attached to those sounds (Moats, 1998).

Exemplary phonics instruction includes the following nine elements:

1. Builds on what a child already knows about how print functions

2. Builds on a child's knowledge of phonemic awareness

3. Is explained in a very clear and direct way

4. Is part of a total, complete reading program

5. Is applied to reading words, not just learning rules

6. May include the instruction of onsets (the syllable part before the vowel) and rimes (the syllable part after the vowel)

7. Could include practice in invented spelling

8. Develops word recognition strategies that enable a child to examine the patterns closely in words

9. Develops word recognition skills that are automatic so that students can concentrate on comprehension, not decoding (Stahl, 1992)

Good phonics instruction should be completed by the end of second grade (Partnership for Reading, 2001).

STRATEGIC ACTIVITIES

Objective: Recognize rhyming words and word families

Brainstorming and Discussion

• Read one of your students' favorite stories from a Big Book for enjoyment. An example would be *Do You Want to Be My Friend?* by Eric Carle. This book is a good choice because it features the repetitive text *Do you want to be my friend?*, as a mouse searches for another animal to be his friend. Select a word from the story, such as the word *be*. Tell students that there are some other words that rhyme with the word "be." These words include *he, she, see, fee,* and *me.* Ask students to brainstorm other words that sound like or rhyme with the word *be.* When students understand the concept of rhyme, select another word from the story and repeat the procedure.

Drawing and Artwork

• Have students make a "Rhyming Words" book by drawing two pictures on each page. The pictures should be of two words that rhyme, such as *man* and *fan* or *toy* and *boy.*

Field Trips

• Take a walk around the school or in the neighborhood. Have students look for objects that rhyme such as *bee* and *tree.*

• Play "I Spy" while on a field trip or neighborhood walk. For example, you could say, "I spy a word that rhymes with class." The students should yell, "grass."

Adaptation: Point to an object on a field trip and have students give you a rhyming word for the word you named.

Games

• Play Concentration by giving two to six students 20 cards (10 rhyming pairs). Have students spread the cards out randomly and face down on a table. Each student takes turns turning over a card and naming the word on the card. The student then turns over another card in an attempt to find a word that rhymes with the word on the card selected. If the rhyme is made, then that student keeps the cards and takes another turn. If not, the turn proceeds to the next player. The student with the most matches at the end of the game wins.

Graphic Organizers, Semantic Maps, and Word Webs

• Write the following word web on the board. Have students complete the map by brainstorming words that rhyme with the word in the middle.

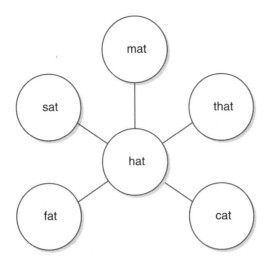

Humor

- Have students solve riddles similar to the following:

    I am used for writing and rhyme with hen. What am I? (Pen)

    I shine in the sky by day and rhyme with fun. What am I? (Sun)

    I am a color and rhyme with shoe? What am I? (Blue)

Manipulatives

- Give each pair of students a sandwich bag containing cards. On five cards are printed word families, such as _an, _ig, _un, _ed, and _op. On the remaining cards are initial consonant letters. Students work together making as many rhyming words as possible by placing initial consonant letters in front of a word family and pronouncing the word. For example, for the word family _an, the student could make *r*an, *c*an, *t*an, and *v*an.

- Use Unifix Letter Cubes to teach letter names, phonic sounds, blends, and word families. Unifix Cubes are rubber blocks that can be manipulated to make words. Have students make as many words as possible by putting the cubes together and pronouncing each word. This activity can be turned into a game by having each student make as many words as possible in a set time limit. Learn more about these manipulatives at www.didaxinc.com.

Movement

- Read pairs of words aloud to the class. Make sure you include pairs of words that rhyme and some that do not. Have students stand up every time you read a pair of words that rhyme and remain seated each time the two words do not rhyme.

- Give some students cards containing word families. Give other students cards with initial consonant letters. Students walk around the room until they find another student whose word card makes a word when added to theirs. For example, a child with an "s" card could pair with a child with the "_un" word family to make the word *sun*.

- Randomly give students word cards. A word is written on each card that rhymes with a word on another card. Each student must find another student with a word card that rhymes with their word card. When found, the students stand together and say their words aloud.

Music, Rhythm, Rhyme, and Rap

- Use music to teach rhyming words by having students sing several of their favorite songs. Following many repetitions, select key rhyming words from the lyrics and have students name the words that rhyme. For example, in the song,

> *Baa, Baa, Black Sheep, Have you any wool?*
> *Yes sir, yes sir, Three bags full*

students could name the rhyming words *wool* and *full*.

- Read a favorite nursery rhyme or poem aloud to the class for enjoyment. During a rereading, have students listen for the rhyming words and name them with you after the rhyme or poem is complete.

- Have students recite songs and chants that have rhyme and rhythm and also teach concepts. Consult the book *Sing a Song of Poetry* by Pinnell and Fountas (2004) for poems and rhymes to teach not only rhyming words but phonemic awareness, phonics, fluency, and content knowledge as well.

- During a whole-class language experience activity or while students work individually, have students create their own raps. Make sure each rap contains rhyming words that students can listen for as their classmates read aloud their original raps.

Objective: Recognize beginning and ending consonant sounds in words

Brainstorming and Discussion

- Introduce the beginning or ending sound of an alphabet letter by naming words that begin or end with that phoneme, such as the words *door*, *dog*, and *desk* for the initial /d/ phoneme. Have students brainstorm other words that begin or end with the same phoneme.

Drawing and Artwork

- Following the teaching of the sound associated with an initial or ending consonant sound, have students draw pictures of words beginning or ending with that sound. For example, after the teaching of the /s/

sound, have students draw pictures with that same sound such as *sun, sit,* and *seven.*

• Following the teaching of the sound associated with an initial or ending consonant sound, have students cut pictures from magazines of words with the same beginning or ending sound. Have them paste the pictures on a piece of construction paper. Combine the pages of construction paper to make a class alphabet book.

Field Trips

• Take your students for a walk around the school or community. As you walk, point out various objects and have students name the beginning or ending consonant sound they hear as you pronounce the name of the object.

Games

• Buy or construct a game board, game pieces, and a die or number wheel. Make game cards containing pictures of objects that begin or end with the sounds you have taught. Have students work in small groups to play the board game according to the following rules. Place the game cards face down in a pile. Students in the group take turns rolling the die or spinning the number wheel, picking a card from the pile, pronouncing the name of the object on the card, and naming the beginning or ending sound of the object. If correct, they move their game piece the same number of spaces as the number rolled on the die or spun on the wheel. If incorrect, their game piece remains where it is on the board. It is then the next student's turn. The first student to reach the end of the game board is the winner.

• Play I Spy by looking around the classroom and saying the following: *I spy a word that begins with the /t/ sound.* The first student to name an object in the classroom that begins with that sound is the winner.

Movement

• Randomly give students letter cards that represent the beginning or ending sounds that they have studied. As you name selected words, have students stand if they have a card that represents the beginning or ending sound of the word named.

Music, Rhythm, Rhyme, and Rap

• Have students sing familiar songs. After enjoying the songs, select key words that contain the beginning or ending sounds you have taught. Have students name the beginning or ending sounds of the words selected. For example, in the song "Old McDonald Had a Farm," have students name the beginning sounds of the names of the animals on the farm.

Reciprocal Teaching and Cooperative Learning

• Have students work with partners to write sentences containing as many words as possible that begin with a selected consonant sound. For example, for the letter /l/, students could write the following sentence: *Linda licks lollipops lying lazily on the land.*

Storytelling

• Following the repeated reading of a favorite story, have students name the beginning or ending sounds of selected words from the story.

• Use alphabet books as read-alouds to reinforce letter-sound recognition. Consult the annotated list of informational alphabet books in the chapter "Sharing Informational Text with Young Children" by Yopp and Yopp (2000).

Visuals

• Place colorful pictures of objects on the wall that represent the various consonant sounds. When students look at these pictures day after day, they are constantly reminded of the relationship between the object and its letter sound.

Writing and Journals

• Examine students' writing or invented spelling for examples of their knowledge of beginning and ending sounds. For example, in a writing sample in which second-graders are asked to write the names of the planets, a student writes the following: *Merkey, Vens, Earth, Mars, Jupeter, Saturn, Uranes, Nursen,* and *Pluto.* The student is obviously applying knowledge of beginning and ending sounds.

Objective: Recognize consonant blends and digraphs

Brainstorming and Discussion

• Following the reading of a story, give students examples of words in the story that begin with consonant blends such as pl, pr, cl, cr, gl, gr, st, sw, or consonant digraphs such as ch, th, sh, wh. Have students brainstorm words that contain each of the consonant blends or digraphs taught.

Games

• Students compete with one another to make the longest or the funniest sentence containing words with consonant blends, digraphs, or both. An example follows: *The cracked crab broke the glad grape.*

Metaphors, Analogies, and Similes

- Have two students come to the front of the room, each carrying one letter of a consonant blend. For example, one student could have the letter /b/ and the other the letter /l/. Have students pronounce each letter sound separately as they stand far apart. Then have the students bring their letter cards and stand as close together as possible. Explain that in some words, two initial consonant sounds "stand as close together as they can." In fact, they stand so close that they blend together. Have students say the sounds rapidly. Explain that these are called consonant blends and that the blend /bl/ sounds like the letters at the beginning of the words *black, blue, block,* and *blister.* Repeat the procedure with other students holding other blends such as /br/, /gr/, /st/, /sw/, /pl/, and /pr/.

Movement

- Randomly give students letter cards that represent the beginning or ending blends or digraphs that have been studied. As you name selected words, have students stand if they have a card that represents the beginning or ending blend or digraph of the word named.

Music, Rhythm, Rhyme, and Rap

- Use music to teach blends or digraphs by having students sing several songs that contain examples. Following many repetitions, select key words from the lyrics and have students name the blend or digraph they hear in each word. For example, in the song "My Country 'Tis of Thee," students could name the first sound they hear in the following words: *Thee, sweet.*

- Have students write a rap or rhyme that contains words with consonant blends or digraphs. Have them read aloud their rap or rhyme to the class and have the class point out the blends and digraphs they hear. An example follows:

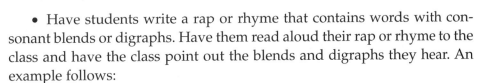

> The pretty princess played in the street.
>
> Until a black bug ran by her feet.
>
> Then, with a thud, she fell to the ground.
>
> But she wasn't hurt. She got up with a frown.

Role Plays, Drama, Pantomimes, and Charades

- Ask two students to come to the front of the class. Pronounce the word *black.* Explain to students that at the beginning of the word *black* are two sounds that like each other very much, so they work together. Name one student the /b/ sound and the other student the /l/ sound. Have the two students stand close together to demonstrate that these two sounds blend together. Pronounce the two sounds blended together and have students do the same /bl/. Have other students come to the front of the room and role play the following additional blended phonemes: /pl/ as in play, /cl/ as in clock, and /fl/ as in flower. When students appear to comprehend blends with the letter /l/, use examples of other blended words such as /br/ in bread, /sk/ as in skate, or /tw/ as in twinkle.

Storytelling

• Read aloud one of the class's favorite stories that contains examples of words with consonant blends or digraphs. Following several readings to enjoy the literature, select key words containing blends or digraphs from the story and have students name the sounds they hear at the beginning of each word.

Objective: Recognize the vowel sounds in words

Drawing and Artwork

• Design a class Vowel Big Book by assigning one short or long vowel letter to each pair of students. The pairs' job is to take a large piece of construction paper and draw and color at least five pictures that all begin with the vowel sound assigned. For example, one pair of students could draw the following short /a/ words: cat, hat, man, bag, and ran. Encourage students to make their drawings as attractive as possible because all drawings will be assembled into a class Big Book for students to share.

Metaphors, Analogies, and Similes

• Select an animal or object with a name that begins with the same initial sound as each vowel. For example:

Short A	Adam Ant	Long A	Amos Ape
Short E	Ella Elephant	Long E	Ealy Eel
Short I	Icabod Iguana	Long I	Ida Iron
Short O	Ollie Octopus	Long O	Opie Oak
Short U	Utley Umbrella	Long U	Usef Unicorn

• Design a graphic containing the vowel letter and a picture of the object. Teach the sounds of the vowels by associating each of them to the object whose name begins with that sound. These become your "vowel characters."

Movement

• Have fun with students by reading a list of words containing short and long vowel sounds. Students stand up if the vowel sound in the word is long because when the human body is standing, it is longer. Students remain seated if the vowel sound in the word is short because the human body is shorter when it is seated.

• Write each separate phoneme of a given word on a large card. Have one student come to the front of the room for each phoneme in the given word. For example, in the word *bed,* have three students come to the front of the room—one for the /b/, one for the /e/, and one for the /d/. Have students pronounce the word made by the three students. Now, change the vowel sound in the word by having the student with the /e/ sit down and substituting another student with another vowel in the same place. For example, the student with the /a/ sound could come forward. Students try to pronounce the new word and tell whether it is a real or nonsense word. Repeat the same procedure with several medial sounds.

• During one of the repeated shared readings of a favorite class story, have students listen for words with the vowel sound being studied. As the word with the appropriate vowel sound is read, have students clap one time. Watch the smiles as students attempt to outdo their classmates and try not to clap at the wrong time!

Music, Rhythm, Rhyme, or Rap

• Create a song that will help students' brains remember the sounds associated with each vowel letter. For example, a song for the short /a/ or the long /e/ sound could be as follows:

> To the tune of "Are You Sleeping" (or "Frere Jacques") students could sing "Are You Acting, Are You Acting, Adam Ant, Adam Ant or "Are You Eating, Are You Eating, Eli Eel, Eli Eel. Morning bells are ringing. Morning bells are ringing. Ding! Dong! Ding!"

• Purchase prerecorded CDs of songs that teach or reinforce reading and language arts skills. For example, on his CD *Shake, Rattle and Read,* Jack Hartmann leads children in singing songs that teach skills from ABCs to vowel sounds. Order Jack Hartmann's CDs at his Web site: www .JackHartmann.com.

• Another person who has numerous songs, rhymes, and chants for teaching reading and language arts skills is Dr. Jean Feldman. Order her CDs at www.drjean.org.

Storytelling

• Select a story to read aloud that has a preponderance of one particular vowel sound such as *Jake Baked a Cake,* which is perfect for teaching or reinforcing the long /a/ sound. Following several readings simply for enjoyment, have students identify key words that contain the long /a/ sound. List the words on the board so that students can look for similarities and differences in spelling patterns.

• Use authentic text to teach students to recognize vowel sounds in words. For example, to reinforce the short /a/ sound, read *The Cat in the Hat* by Dr. Seuss; To reinforce the long /a/ sound, *Bringing the Rain to Kapiti Plain* by Verna Aardema is great.

Visuals

• Post the "vowel characters" (created in the metaphor activity or purchased prepackaged) on the wall as a constant reminder of the sounds associated with each vowel sound.

Writing and Journals

• Have students write a story containing words that represent a particular vowel pattern, such as short vowel words.

REFLECTION AND APPLICATION

> ## Which strategies can I use to teach phonics so that my students' brains are engaged?

Standard/Objective: _____

_____

_____.

Activity: _____

_____

_____.

Standard/Objective: _____

_____

_____.

Activity: _____

_____

_____.

Standard/Objective: _____

_____

_____.

Activity: _____

_____

_____.

Standard/Objective: _____

_____

_____.

Activity: _____

_____

_____.

Standard/Objective: _____

_____

_____.

Activity: _____

_____

_____.

3

Fluency

Students who read and reread passages orally increase speed, accuracy, and fluency.

—Partnership for Reading, 2001

Have you ever listened as a person read orally in a monotone, laborious fashion? In no time at all, you began to lose interest in what was being read, and your comprehension was probably nonexistent. This reader lacked fluency and, besides that, probably had little or no understanding of what was just read.

The term "fluency" has been defined in a variety of ways including "the freedom from word identification problems that might hinder comprehension (Harris & Hodges, 1995); the ability to read rapidly (Hirsch, 2003); or the ability to read at a rate appropriate for accuracy, smoothness, phrasing, expressiveness, and intonation (Anderson, 2004). Fluent readers are capable of concentrating their efforts on comprehension because they are able to make connections between the ideas presented in the text and their own background knowledge. Readers who are not as fluent have little time left for comprehending because all of their efforts go toward decoding separate words (Partnership for Reading, 2001). After all, the research tells us that the brain can only pay conscious attention to one thing at a time. If that constant thing is decoding individual words, then little time and effort can be used understanding what is being read.

As a reading specialist, it used to surprise me that many of my students were capable of reading words accurately and quickly from a list but were not nearly as fluent when reading those same words within the context of a passage or story. Research tells us that fluency is not constant for a reader but changes based not only on familiarity with the words but on the text and the number of repetitions. For example, a student who has no difficulty reading a novel of interest with expression and automaticity may have less ease dealing with the text from a highly technical manual or physics book.

Although experts agree that increases in fluency result from practicing the act of reading, there is disagreement on the form that practice should take. One technique for developing fluency is to ask students to read and reread passages aloud with support and feedback (National Reading Panel, 2000). Explicit programs that support this approach include shared, paired, and assisted reading along with repeated readings and the neurological impress method described in this chapter. Repeated oral reading appears to increase the reading ability of all elementary students as well as those readers who need help at upper grade levels. Customarily having students read and reread the same text at least four times tends to improve fluency (Partnership for Reading, 2001). Therefore you will find multiple examples of repeated reading activities in the pages that follow.

Round-robin oral reading, a practice widely used in many classrooms, does not appear to qualify as one of the techniques that increase fluency (Partnership for Reading, 2001). This is probably because students are only reading small amounts of text and usually only once. In addition, if you really think about it, few students are actually listening when others are reading in round-robin fashion. If they are smart, then they will be counting down the paragraphs or pages to determine when their time to read is coming, and they may be practicing so that they can sound fluent on at least that small part of text.

A different, yet widely embraced, approach is to engage students in reading consistently, yet independently, with little teacher guidance or feedback. Programs that support this alternative approach include DEAR (*Drop Everything and Read*) Time, SSR (sustained silent reading), and other incentive programs such as Accelerated Reader.

Chapman and King (2003) delineated a number of elements for developing a fluent reader. These include exposing the reader to enthusiastic, expressive models of reading; using meaningful activities before, during, and after reading to develop understanding; using a variety of active engagement strategies; and engaging the student in high-interest reading materials written on an appropriate level.

When teachers read orally and naturally to their students, they serve as models of fluent oral reading. When they point the students' attention to the way they are reading, they help students understand that the message is carried not just in the words that are read but also in the expressions used when reading the words (Rasinski, 2003).

RELEVANT RESEARCH

Fluency can be built in the following four ways: (a) by modeling good oral reading, (b) by providing oral support for a student's reading ability, (c) by providing many opportunities for the student to practice, and (d) by encouraging students to chunk or phrase the text appropriately (Rasinski, 2003).

Repeated oral readings, rather than silent ones, give extrasensory input to the student, providing opportunities to concentrate on those elements necessary for proper phrasing (Rasinski, 2003).

When students engage in readers' theatre, they improve fluency because multiple repetitions of the text during practice increases automaticity and enable the students to take on the expressiveness of the characters they portray (Martinez, Roser, & Strecker, 2002).

Students who read and reread passages orally not only improve word recognition but also increase their speed, accuracy, and fluency (Partnership for Reading, 2001).

Some students require as many as 14 to 20 repetitions of a word to become totally fluent with that word (McEwan, 2001).

Techniques that appear effective for increasing fluency include approximately four rereadings of the same text, the use of audiotapes, peer coaching, and tutors (Partnership for Reading, 2001).

Although silent, independent reading can be beneficial for practice, it in no way takes the place of direct instruction (Partnership for Reading, 2001).

According to the National Assessment of Educational Progress, 44% of a sample of fourth graders were not fluent in their reading ability (Partnership for Reading, 2001).

Students who have difficulty with fluency may also have problems comprehending what they read (National Reading Panel, 2000).

Guided oral reading procedures with feedback have a positive and consistent impact on fluency as well as word recognition and comprehension at a variety of grade levels (National Reading Panel, 2000).

Students who are unable to develop reading fluency, regardless of their intellect, will continue to expend great effort and read very slowly (National Reading Panel, 2000).

There was no evidence to support the effectiveness of independent silent reading as a method for improving reading performance (National Reading Panel, 2000).

To develop fluency, some students need consistent drill with the 1,000 most frequently occurring words until they can recognize these words instantly by sight (Fry, 1999).

Students cannot make adequate progress learning to read if they do not receive adequate practice in achieving fluency within the context of various texts (Snow, Burns, & Griffin, 1998).

In a New Zealand study, students listened to books on tape while simultaneously reading a printed version of the same text for 20 to 30 minutes daily. Students repeated the procedure until they felt they could read the book on their own and then moved to the next more difficult passage. After three fourths of a school year, reading achievement gains tripled those anticipated (Smith & Elley, 1997).

For students to become fluent with a word, they must consciously process the sounds and letter patterns of the word during the initial few times that it is read (Share & Stanovich, 1995).

Comprehension improves when a student reads text and hears a simultaneous fluent rendition of the same text (Topping, 1995).

In a 1995 study of more than 1,000 fourth graders, the most fluent students also had the best comprehension following both oral and silent reading (Pinnell et al., 1995).

Students don't even begin to experience fluency until they have learned between 15,000 and 20,000 words (d'Anna, Zechmeister, & Hall, 1991).

Good readers use their knowledge of letter-sound relationships to enable them to read words in isolation but also are capable of processing print quickly and discerning the meaning (Nicholson, 1991).

It is necessary for students to learn the meanings of 3,000 new vocabulary words annually if they are to become fluent readers (Nagy, 1988).

Students in low reading groups in a classroom often receive few opportunities to practice fluency because they read as few as 16 words in a week. Those students in higher reading groups could read almost 2,000 words per week (Allington, 1984).

STRATEGIC ACTIVITIES

Objective: Improve students' automaticity and fluency with text

Brainstorming and Discussion

• Select an appropriate text for the purpose of choral reading. This text may be from a song, poem, class motto, or favorite part of a story. Have all students attempt to read the text aloud simultaneously. Because some students will read the text with more fluency than others, those who need it will benefit from hearing the fluent voices of others. Have students reread the same text several times and discuss how they felt during each rereading. Some questions to be asked include the following:

How did you feel about your reading during each repetition?

Do you think your reading performance improved?

Do you understand what you just read?

Can you tell me about what you read?

Games

• Play *Beat the Clock* by having students take turns reading as many high-frequency (sight) words as they can from a designated list within a 1-minute time period. Each student attempts to beat his or her previous individual score by increasing the number of words read.

• Play the *Fluency Game* by setting a timer for one minute. Have one student read a familiar passage until the timer goes off. Have another student count the number of words read correctly by the first student within the one-minute time limit. Set the timer again. Have the first student reread the same passage for the purpose of increasing the number of words read correctly. It is now the second student's turn. The student in each pair who increases his or her score by the largest number of words read correctly in a minute is the winner of the game.

Humor

• Read a portion of a favorite story aloud to the class. As you begin reading, read the story very slowly, in a monotone voice, with no expression, no interest, and no enjoyment. Ask students how they felt listening to you read aloud. Explain to students that reading is the same as talking. It is simply the words the author would say written down in print. Ask some of the following questions to the students: *How did you feel about this story? Were you interested in what I had to say? If I asked you questions about the story, would you be able to answer them?* Tell students that the more they read, the better they'll read and that you are expecting them to read with expression and interest.

Manipulatives

• Put phrases from a familiar class story on sentence strips so that students can focus on phrases rather than individual words. Pass out the sentence strips to students and have them practice reading them silently and aloud. Students can exchange sentence strips with one another and practice reading the new strips aloud.

• Assist students in identifying, highlighting, reading, and rereading meaningful phrases in text.

Metaphors, Analogies, and Similes

• Explain to students that reading is like talking and that the words on a page are the writer's thoughts and actions written down. Therefore, when people read, they must read as if they were speaking to another person. Explain how this concept relates to fluency. Model read a passage fluently for students.

Music, Rhythm, Rhyme, and Rap

• Use music to teach fluency by having students sing and then recite the lyrics to a familiar song or rap. Print the lyrics so that all students can read them with proper intonation and phrasing.

• Use familiar, funny, or motivational poems and rhymes with students. Give students a copy of the poems or rhymes to be read. Read the poems aloud to the students several times for enjoyment. Then, to improve fluency, involve students in a choral rereading of the poems or rhymes.

Project-Based and Problem-Based Instruction

• Have older students read aloud a book at their independent reading level to students in a lower grade level. To determine whether a book is at a student's independent reading level, have the student read a sample passage of 100 words. If the student can read an average of 95 of the 100 words correctly, then the passage is on the appropriate level. To prepare to read the book with expression, the reader will need to engage in repeated oral readings of the text, thereby improving his or her fluency.

• Purchase prerecorded books or stories on tape or create them for the class. Have students listen to the story read fluently on tape while tracking the words in the accompanying text. After repeated opportunities to listen, have students read along softly with the tape, modeling the expression and fluency exhibited on the tape.

• *Read Naturally,* a program developed by Candyce Ihnot, a Title I reading specialist, appears successful for improving fluency. For one minute, have students read text written at their instructional level. (Instructional level is defined at the point at which a student can recognize 90% to 95% of the words and answer at least 75% of the comprehension questions related to the passage.) Students then reread the same passage at least three or four times while simultaneously listening to a recording of the passage. When students feel as if they can read the passage on their own, as determined by program guidelines, they proceed to a more difficult text, and the process is repeated.

• Participate with students in structured opportunities to read independently by providing SSR or DEAR Time. These activities enable both adults and students to spend uninterrupted time reading self-selected books.

• Incorporate the Accelerated Reading Program into your curriculum according to program guidelines. Students select books of appropriate readability. They read these books independently and take online comprehension test to ascertain whether they comprehended what they read. Students are rewarded for reaching predetermined goals and proceed to books with more difficult readability.

Reciprocal Teaching and Cooperative Learning

• Have students work in pairs reading and rereading familiar text in a story they have previously read. Keith Topping (1995) found that when a fluent reader (the tutor) is paired with a less fluent reader, the latter's fluency improves. His procedure is as follows: Have students sit beside one another with a text selected by the less fluent reader. The pair read together for approximately 10 to 20 minutes, with the tutor matching his or her reading voice to that of the student. Whenever the student makes an error, the tutor quickly corrects it so that the flow of the reading is not disrupted. If the student chooses to read without the assistance of the tutor, this wish is respected; however, the tutor jumps in whenever the student errs.

• Engage students in the *neurological impress method*, a technique developed by Heckelman in 1969, according to the following procedure: As in paired reading, have two students work together, with the better reader acting as the tutor. The text should be written on the instructional level of the student who is not serving as the tutor. The tutor and the student read the same text, with the tutor reading slightly faster than the student. The tutor's voice should be directed into the student's left ear to "imprint" a match from sound to symbol. Because of the intense nature of this technique, the initial sessions should last only a few minutes, with the time slowly extended to sessions of no more than 15 minutes.

• Have students read and reread aloud passages from a familiar book to a parent, guardian, or other adult until the student reads the passages with ease. The adult should also serve as a model of fluent oral reading, helping the student with unfamiliar words and giving feedback related to the student's reading performance.

Role Plays, Drama, Pantomimes, and Charades

• Have students engage in readers' theatre by rehearsing and performing a play created from a book with much dialogue. Readers' theatre is performed by a narrator who provides the setting of the story and other background information and characters who speak the dialogue.

• Select books that are already written in script format so that it is easy for students to participate in the repeated readings inherent in readers' theatre. Consult the list of script books and the list of easy, moderately challenging, and challenging books that can be recast as scripts found on page 164 of the book *From Phonics to Fluency* by Rasinski and Padak (2001).

Storytelling

• Be certain that whenever you are reading aloud to the class, you serve as the best model of oral reading fluency. Read with appropriate phrasing, expression, and intonation.

• Model fluency by reading aloud a story from a Big Book, an enlarged copy of a children's book. Make sure that all students can see the text, and point to each word as you read. Show students how to "chunk text" into meaningful phrases. Explain at which points you are pausing and why you use different voice inflections.

• Read aloud one of the class's favorite stories. Following several readings simply for enjoyment of the literature, have students take turns reading and rereading short passages to improve fluency.

• Have students read and reread texts that develop phonemic awareness and fluency because they either contain rhyming words or words that play with sounds. Sample texts would include the following: *A, My Name Is Alice* by J. Bayor; *I Can't, Said the Ant* by P. Cameron; *The Cat in the Hat* and *Green Eggs and Ham* by T. S. Geisel (Dr. Seuss); *Read Aloud Rhymes for the Very Young* by J. Prelutsky; and *Richard Scarry's Best Mother Goose Ever* by R. Scarry. An extensive list of books that develop phonemic awareness can be found on pages 36 and 37 of *From Phonics to Fluency* by Rasinski and Padak (2001).

• Have students read and reread books with predictable patterned texts because students can easily catch on to the repetitive text and improve their fluency through repeated readings. Sample predictable books include *Goodnight Moon* and *The Important Book* by M. W. Brown, *The Very Hungry Caterpillar* by Eric Carle, *Hattie and the Fox* by Mem Fox, and *Rosie's Walk* and *The Doorbell Rang* by Pat Hutchins. A more complete list of predictable books can be found on pages 17 and 18 of *From Phonics to Fluency* by Rasinski and Padak (2001).

Visuals

• Provide students with videotapes that contain familiar songs and their accompanying lyrics, which often run along the television screen. Have students listen to the songs and read or sing along with the lyrics. Once students are fluent with the lyrics, print them on sentence strips or word cards and have students read them without the recording.

• Select a passage from a story that students have read and reread. Embed slash marks in the passage at specific points to encourage students to read in phrases rather than word-by-word because they are not to pause or take a breath until they get to a slash mark. The slash marks provide visual cues that encourage proper phrasing.

• Have students select a television show that has closed captions. While listening to the show's dialogue, students have the opportunity to see the printed text appearing on the bottom of the television screen.

Writing and Journals

• Engage students in a whole-class language experience activity by assisting them in writing an original story based on an adaptation of a favorite children's book. For example, the class story *If You Give a Mouse a Slice of Pizza* could be based on the children's story *If You Give a Mouse a Cookie.* Give each student a copy of the class story and have them read and reread it to improve fluency.

REFLECTION AND APPLICATION

> ## Which strategies can I use to teach fluency so that my students' brains are engaged?

Standard/Objective: _____

_____

_____.

Activity: _____

_____

_____.

Standard/Objective: _____

_____

_____.

Activity: _____

_____

_____.

Standard/Objective: _____

_____

_____.

Activity: _____

_____

_____.

Standard/Objective: _____

_____

_____.

Activity: _____

_____

_____.

Standard/Objective: _____

_____

_____.

Activity: _____

_____

_____.

Vocabulary Instruction

4

Vocabulary instruction is often a product of a variety of opportunities to learn.

—Blachowicz & Fisher, 2002

Vocabulary appears crucial in learning to read. In fact, deficits in the vocabulary of disadvantaged students seem to be one the primary causes of academic failure (Anderson, 2004). There appear to be mixed results, however, regarding exactly how crucial it is to teach vocabulary separate from comprehension. Recent research appears to place more emphasis on the total act of comprehension rather than vocabulary instruction alone (Report of the National Reading Panel, 2000).

There are various categories of vocabulary. Receptive vocabulary refers to those words that can be understood by the learner when others are speaking or writing. Productive or expressive vocabulary refers to those words the learner uses with facility when personally speaking or writing (McEwan, 2001). The activities contained in this chapter reinforce both types of vocabulary development.

A teacher cannot and should not teach all unfamiliar words in a text for the following reasons: (a) the number of unfamiliar words may be too numerous or time-consuming to teach; (b) not every unfamiliar word is crucial to a student's comprehension of the text, and (c) students need opportunities to use vocabulary strategies to learn words on their own (Partnership for Reading, 2001).

Research also relates that fluency can be enhanced through the instant recognition of between 200 and 300 high-frequency words. These words, also referred to as "basic sight words," are crucial for good readers because they appear to comprise more than 50% of all the words a reader will ever experience. Although high-frequency words seem to be simple to master, this is not always the case. High-frequency words can be difficult for several reasons. First, many of these words have little or no meaning attached to them unless they are contained within the context of other words. For example, what is an *if,* an *of,* or a *that*? You can't draw a picture of one, nor can you easily explain the definition to someone else. Second, so many of the words have similar letter configurations. Students often have a difficult time distinguishing the words *what* and *want* or *who* and *how.* Lastly, many high-frequency words are not phonetic. Conventional letter-sound associations simply don't work. For example, *come* should phonetically rhyme with *home* or *what* with *that.* Despite these inconsistencies, teaching and reinforcing high-frequency words is time well spent. A word of caution is in order, however. The teaching and reinforcing of too many sight words during the formative years can limit the reader's ability to acquire the orthographic rules necessary for decoding (Wolfe & Nevills, 2004).

Delineated below are strategies that should be used for teaching and reinforcing high-frequency words. These same 20 brain-compatible strategies can also be employed to teach the concepts necessary for expanding both receptive and expressive vocabularies. Once students have had an opportunity to role play, story tell, and brainstorm their way to vocabulary acquisition, gains in comprehension and reading achievement should occur.

RELEVANT RESEARCH

Having students recognize 200–300 sight words from memory at a very early age can encourage "automaticity of common words" (Teele, 2004).

Developing vocabulary and teaching spelling words within the context of literature assists students in understanding word meanings (Teele, 2004).

Students with excellent memory skills for sight words may have difficulty when attempting to read text with multisyllabic words if they have not developed decoding strategies as well (Wolfe & Nevills, 2004).

Techniques that were once solely used to teach high-frequency words in the primary grades are now being used to teach vocabulary across the curriculum (Bender, 2003).

Vocabulary instruction is not always a result of direct teacher instruction. It can often be a product of a variety of opportunities to learn (Blachowicz & Fisher, 2002).

Three best practices recommended for effective vocabulary instruction include the following: (1) enable students to use both definition and context in learning new words, (2) allow students to cognitively use the new words, and (3) engage students in constant conversation about the new words (McEwan, 2001).

Creating a positive environment for learning vocabulary includes incorporating materials and activities that enable students to actually play with words (Blachowicz & Fisher, 2002).

When two students collaborate on a research project, an English-as-a-second-language student can learn as much vocabulary as during a more structured vocabulary lesson (Blachowicz & Fisher, 2002).

Although some vocabulary should be taught directly, students learn most new vocabulary indirectly through conversations with adults, being read to, and reading widely on their own (Partnership for Reading, 2001).

Students learn vocabulary best when they are actively engaged with words over an extended period of time (Partnership for Reading, 2001).

The four types of word learning include the following: (1) learning a new or different meaning for a word already known, (2) learning the meaning for a new word when the concept is already known, (3) clarifying or enriching the meaning of a word already known, and (4) the most difficult, learning the meaning of a new word that represents a concept that is not already known (Partnership for Reading, 2001).

Students learn more words indirectly through real-life experiences with both oral and written language (National Reading Panel, 2000).

Highly technical or subject-specific vocabulary can be learned through teacher-directed instruction (National Reading Panel, 2000).

To enhance memory and deep processing of vocabulary words, students need many opportunities to use the words in listening, speaking, reading, and writing activities (Rupley et al., 1999).

Language experience is one of the best ways to teach sight words to beginning readers as well as to older remedial students who recognize a limited number of sight words (Towell, 1998).

Fourth- and fifth-grade students who were pretaught vocabulary appeared to have greater gains in vocabulary acquisition (Brett, Rothlein, & Hurley, 1996).

Compelling research suggests that reading aloud to students of all ages is beneficial to vocabulary acquisition (Dickinson & Smith, 1994; Robbins & Ehri, 1994).

The amount of student talk and active student participation is important for gains in vocabulary achievement (Dickinson & Smith, 1994).

> Students must actively process vocabulary in a variety of contexts if it is to be easily retrieved (Marzano & Marzano, 1988).
>
> To make vocabulary instruction meaningful, words should be taught in categories or clusters, with related synonyms or words associated with the key word (Marzano & Marzano, 1988).
>
> When college students used their vocabulary words to write songs, their vocabulary knowledge improved (Baechtold & Algiers, 1986).
>
> The use of analogies deepens students' understanding of abstract concepts and content area material by connecting new information with known information (Kuse & Kuse, 1986).
>
> Allowing students to sing during vocabulary instruction enables them to use both hemispheres of the brain, particularly the right hemisphere (Guglielmino, 1986).
>
> Comprehension comprises both vocabulary or knowledge of words and one's ability to reason while reading (Davis, 1942).

STRATEGIC ACTIVITIES

Objective: Identify high-frequency vocabulary words in texts

Drawing and Artwork

• Have students dictate sentences using high-frequency words in context. Write the sentence and have the student draw a picture to accompany it.

Games

• Construct or buy a game board, a number generator (die), and markers. Place the high-frequency words to be learned on index cards. Have two to five students compete against one another by rolling the number generator. To move the rolled number of spaces, the student must select from the pile and name the same number of sight words. If the student names all of the words, the student moves that number of spaces on the game board. If the student misses a word, the student can only move one space for each word correctly named. The first student to get to the end of the game board wins.

• Write matching pairs of 15 high-frequency words to be learned on index cards. Turn them face down and spread them out randomly. Have students compete in pairs to locate the matching high-frequency words. The student must name each word selected. When a matching pair is made, the student names the word, keeps the cards, and is allowed to get another turn. When all pairs are matched, the student with the most matches wins.

Manipulatives

• Have students manipulate magnetic letters to spell out designated high-frequency words. The magnetic letters can adhere to a magnetic cookie sheet or a metal file cabinet.

• Have students spell out high-frequency words in shaving cream spread on their desks.

• Have students spell out high-frequency words in a salt or sand tray.

• Have students use a multisensory technique to trace a high-frequency word with the finger while pronouncing each syllable until that word can be written from memory.

• Have students write high-frequency words in the air or on the back of another student.

Metaphors, Analogies, and Similes

• Teach unfamiliar high-frequency words by comparing them to words the student already knows. For example, in teaching the word *know*, tell students that it begins like the word *knot*. Show a picture of a knot so that students can tie the pronunciation of the two words together.

Movement

• Place laminated, high-frequency words on the floor in a path. As students walk the path, they must name the word on which they are about to step. When a student misses a word, he or she must go back to the beginning of the path and start again.

Music, Rhythm, Rhyme, and Rap

• Select familiar songs or rhymes that have high-frequency words in the lyrics such as the ones underlined in the song below:

> Twinkle, twinkle, <u>little</u> star
>
> <u>How</u> <u>I</u> wonder <u>what</u> <u>you</u> <u>are</u>

As students sing the song, point out specific high-frequency words. Have students point to designated words.

• Have students clap out the syllables in multisyllabic high-frequency words.

Reciprocal Teaching and Cooperative Learning

- Have students read and reread books with repetitive texts and high-frequency words aloud to a partner. An example of repetitive books would be *Brown Bear, Brown Bear* or *Do You Want to be My Friend?* by Eric Carle.

Role Plays, Drama, Pantomimes, and Charades

- Have students role play, or act out, those basic sight words that have meaning and attempt to get their classmates to guess the words (such as *like, go, play, work*).

Storytelling

- Have students work together to develop a language experience story based on a common theme such as writing the student-generated story *Pink Pig, Pink Pig*, based on the story *Brown Bear, Brown Bear*. As students dictate their story, write it on the board. Use the story to teach the high-frequency words it contains.

Visualization and Guided Imagery

- Have students visualize the spelling of high-frequency words as they write the words in the air.

Visuals

- Place magnetic letters randomly on the overhead so that the entire class can see them. Select a student to come to the overhead and make the designated high-frequency word.

- Place high-frequency words on the wall for students to refer to when writing.

Writing and Journals

- Have students dictate or write a language experience story. By the very nature of a story, high-frequency words will be included. Have students locate and circle or underline selected words.

Objective: Expand students' receptive and expressive vocabularies

Brainstorming and Discussion

- Before students read a story or content-area text, select vocabulary words that will be key to comprehension but that you believe students will have difficulty defining. Place each word on chart paper or an overhead and have students brainstorm or discuss possible definitions for each word. Keep the brainstormed definitions and compare them to the definitions used in the selection.

• Using a word web, have students brainstorm other words that are synonyms for a key word. List students' synonyms on the board or chart paper. Review synonyms whenever the key word is used so that alternative words are connected together in the brain. (Refer to Graphic Organizers later in the chapter for a sample word web.)

• Have students work in pairs to discuss the definitions of assigned vocabulary words. Have them quiz one another on the definitions, stating them in their own words rather than trying to memorize a dictionary definition.

• Read sections of narrative or content-area text aloud. Provide opportunities for students to discuss the definitions of unfamiliar words, perhaps from the context clues provided in the text.

• Engage students in numerous opportunities to read for information and enjoyment. Use books written on each student's instructional level where they can recognize at least 90%–95% of the words. Allow students to discuss their books with classmates. Reading a wide variety of material increases familiarity with many new words.

• Have students work in cooperative groups to brainstorm and write as many vocabulary words as possible pertaining to a particular category, such as words that begin with the letter a, words that are verbs, or words that have prefixes or suffixes.

• Have students use context clues to identify an unknown word by following the procedure outlined before:

1. Place a transparency on the overhead containing a passage with several key vocabulary words omitted. These words should be figured out contextually.

2. Ask students to look at a key word and the words before and after the key word. Have them connect what they already know to what they are reading. Have them predict a probable meaning and make a decision as to whether the meaning fits the context.

3. Discuss the meaning derived and whether it fits the context.

4. Reveal the original word choice of the author and compare it with students' recommendations (adapted from Blachowicz & Fisher, 2002, p. 29).

• Following a unit of study, have students create an alphabet book by brainstorming as many words as they can recall which begin with a designated letter of the alphabet. For example, a math alphabet book could contain the following words:

A	arithmetic, algorithm, algebra
B	binomial, binary, bisect
C	calculus, calculator, communicative property
D	divide, denominator, decimal
E	equal sign, equation, estimate
F	figure, fraction, Fibonacci
G	geometry, geoboard, grams
H	height, hexagon, hectometer

And the list continues.

This "alphabet book" technique can be used with any content area or for any unit of study. It is a way to connect important vocabulary within a meaningful context.

 ## Drawing and Artwork

• Have students draw pictures that illustrate the definitions of key vocabulary words.

• Have students design picture cards for any key vocabulary words that they find difficult to remember. Students can keep their cards in a personal file box or sandwich bag and should review them periodically.

• Have students make collages by cutting specific categories of words from newspapers or magazines. For example, students could make a verb or adjective collage.

• Have students design an original book for teaching vocabulary words indicative of figurative language. Students would illustrate both the literal and the figurative meaning of each word. For example, for the idiom *She knocked me off my feet,* students could draw a girl knocking a boy to the ground and then a second picture of the boy being very impressed by the girl.

• Have students play the game Pictionary according to the following directions: Select key vocabulary terms that you wish them to remember and place each word on a separate index card. Students take turns coming to the front of the class, selecting a word card, and drawing a picture on chart paper or on the board that will enable their classmates to guess the word selected. This activity also utilizes the Games strategy if students score one point when they are the first to guess the given word.

• Have students illustrate the various meanings of a multiple-meaning word. For example, for the word *run,* students could draw the following:

run the race

run for re-election

run her mouth

run in your stocking

• Have students remember a word's meaning by drawing word pictures. A sample follows:

elongated

succinct

Field Trips

• Prior to a field trip, use appropriate brain strategies from the list of 20 to preteach vocabulary words that will be crucial to students' understanding of what will be experienced on the excursion.

Games

• Play Bingo by having students draw a 3 × 3 matrix on their paper. This will give them space in which they can randomly write any nine words from a list of 20–30 designated vocabulary words to be reviewed.

Place the definition of each vocabulary word on the list in a container. Have students take turns pulling a definition from the container and reading it aloud. If any student has written the word that accompanies the definition read, the student draws a circle around the word. When a student has three words in a row (either vertically, horizontally, or diagonally) or when a student has covered four corners of the matrix, the student shouts *"Bingo!"* The first student to do so is the winner and begins the next game by reading the first definition.

• Construct or buy a game board, a number generator (die), and markers. Place key vocabulary words to be learned on index cards. Have two to five students compete against one another by rolling the number generator. To move the rolled number of spaces, the student must select from the pile and name the same number of vocabulary words. If the student names all of the words, the student moves that number of spaces on the game board. If the student misses a word, he or she can only move one space for each word correctly named. The first student to get to the end of the game board wins.

• Write matching pairs of 15 vocabulary words to be learned on index cards. Turn them face down and spread them out randomly. Have students compete in pairs to locate the matching words. The student must turn two cards face up and name each word selected. When a matching pair is made, the student keeps the cards and is allowed to take another turn. When all pairs are matched, the student with the most matches wins.

• Have students play the game Pictionary according to the following directions: Select key vocabulary terms that you wish students to remember and place each word on a separate index card. Students are divided into two or three teams and compete against one another to guess the word their teammate selects. The team that guesses their word in the shortest amount of time in each round wins the round. The team that wins the most rounds wins the overall game.

• Have students make as many smaller words as possible in a designated time period out of the letters in a word written on the board. For example, students have five minutes to make as many words as they can out of the word *combustible.* Possible words might be the following: *combust, comb, come, bus, some, but, let, stile, mob, me, bomb,* and *must.* The student who makes the most real words in the allotted time wins the game.

• Have students play commercial games that reinforce vocabulary acquisition such as Scrabble, Tribond, Upwords, or Scattergories.

Graphic Organizers, Semantic Maps, and Word Webs

• Use the following word web to increase vocabulary by categorizing or clustering synonyms or antonyms to a given word. Write the key word in the middle and have students brainstorm synonyms or antonyms related to the key word. Students keep a notebook containing their graphic organizers and add other related synonyms or antonyms as the year progresses.

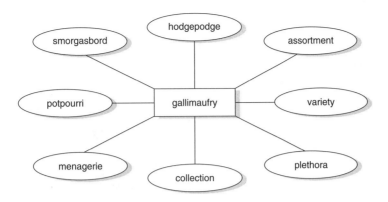

• Have students design character maps as one way students can use vocabulary to describe characters and connect their relationship to the story. An example of a character map follows:

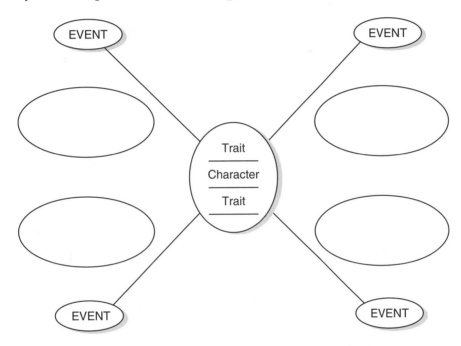

• Have students make a web consisting of words and their roots to expand their knowledge of word meaning. A root word web follows.

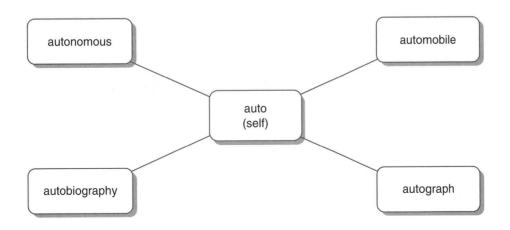

Humor

• Engage students in motivational activities such as the creation of *sniglets*. The term sniglet was coined by Rich Hall and is a made-up word that probably should be in the dictionary but is not there yet. For example, the word *hozone* is a sniglet. The *hozone* can be defined *as the place where one sock in every laundry load goes when it disappears during the wash cycle*. Have students create original sniglets and watch how highly motivated they will be to share them with classmates.

• Have students make up *Tom Swifties*, which are created when a quotation is written followed by an adjective or verb that is in some way related to the quotation. For example, *I wish I could be more like you*, said Nancy vicariously or *I sure am hungry*, said John voraciously. Tom Swifties are named for Tom Swift, a fictional character who used these sayings in several books written by Edward Stratemeyer in the early 1900s.

• Have students create word riddles using the following procedure:

1. Select a subject (such as dog).

2. Formulate a list of words related to the subject (such as bark, bite).

3. Select a word (such as bark) and eliminate the initial letter to shorten the word (such as ark) and find a list of words that begin just like the shortened version (such as ark, Arkansas).

4. Put the missing letter back (b) (Barkansas).

5. Develop riddles for which the word can be the answer. For example, In which state was the dog born? Barkansas! (Blachowicz & Fisher, 2002).

• Have each student create a *Hink Pink*, a pair of one-syllable rhyming words that match a phrase that defines the word. For example, *pedicured appendages* would be *neat feet*. For additional challenge, have each student create a *Hinky Pinky*, a pair of two-syllable rhyming words that match a phrase that defines the word. For example, *a mysterious woman* is a *shady lady*. Each student who is up to the task could create a Hinkety Pinkety, a pair of three-syllable rhyming words, the most challenging pair in this activity. For example, a malfunctioning part of speech is a *dysfunction conjunction*.

• Teach students the use of figurative language by asking them to complete some well-known proverbs. For example, give students the stem of the proverb and have them complete the stem. Then discuss the actual proverb and its literal and figurative meaning. Some possible proverbs are as follows:

It's always darkest before . . .

Don't bite the hand that . . .

You can't teach an old dog new . . .

A penny saved is . . .

Children should be seen and not . . .

A bird in the hand is worth . . .

Manipulatives

• Have students manipulate magnetic letters to spell out designated vocabulary words. The magnetic letters can adhere to a magnetic cookie sheet or a metal file cabinet.

• Have students spell out vocabulary words in shaving cream spread on their desks.

• Have students spell out vocabulary words in a salt or sand tray.

• Have students use a multisensory technique to trace a vocabulary word with the finger while pronouncing each syllable until that word can be written from memory.

• Have students write vocabulary words in the air or on the back of another student.

• Have students write words on sentence strips and then cut them into word parts (e.g., prefixes, suffixes, syllables). Students mix up the word parts and then reassemble them into the original words or make new ones.

• Give students freezer bags containing cards with vocabulary words that have been taught and need to be reviewed. Have students work individually or with a partner to lay the cards out in groups according to student-selected categories. For example, students may want to group all the verbs together, or all the words that describe (adjectives), or all the words that represent a place (noun). The categories are numerous. Use informal observation to check accuracy.

• Have students form a synonym and antonym continuum. Pass out word cards to students. Each word occupies a place on a continuum. Have students come to the front of the class and place themselves in the order of the continuum. A sample follows:

ecstatic	joyful	happy	indifferent	angry	furious

Metaphors, Analogies, and Similes

• When teaching new vocabulary words, compare them to words the students already know. For example, tell students that the word *knout* (which means a whip) begins like some other words they already know, such as *knowledge, knee, knot,* and *knight.*

• Have students engage in Glynn's *TWA (Teaching with Analogies)* approach by following the procedure outlined below:

1. Introduce the concept to be learned.

2. Review a familiar but similar concept through the use of analogy.

3. Identify the features of both the new and known concept.

4. Explain what both concepts have in common.

5. Explain how the new concept is different from the known. (At this point the analogy breaks down.)

6. Draw conclusions regarding the major ideas that students need to remember about the new concept (Glynn, 1996).

Mnemonic Devices

• Teach students the steps outlined in the *IT FITS* strategy to master the meanings of new words. The steps are as follows:

7. *Identify* the vocabulary word

8. *Tell* the word's definition

9. *Find* a related word for the vocabulary word

10. *Imagine* a picture of the vocabulary word

11. *Think* about the definition as it relates to the vocabulary word

12. *Study* what you imagined until you can easily recall the definition

Movement

• Have students "body spell" by standing and raising their hands above their heads if the letter goes above the line; extending their arms out to their sides if the letter is on the line, and bending at the waist and stretching their arms toward the floor if the letter dips below the line. For example, to spell the word "play," students would bend down for the "p" and "y," up for the "l," and out to the sides for the "a" as they say each letter in order.

• Provide a movement or action to depict appropriate vocabulary words to be learned. Students stand and model the movement as you name the word and demonstrate the action. For example, for the word *amble,* students get up and walk across the floor.

Music, Rhythm, Rhyme, and Rap

• Have students work individually or in groups to create songs or raps that connect the vocabulary words to be learned with their meanings.

• Have students work individually or in groups to create rhymes or poems that will help them remember the definitions of key vocabulary terms.

• Have students clap out a variety of word parts such as the syllables in each word or the affixes of a root word.

Project-Based and Problem-Based Instruction

• Have students create personal word banks for storing and recalling both their self-selected and teacher-selected words. Throughout the year, these word banks will grow, instilling self-confidence in students' ability to add new words to their reading, writing, listening, and speaking vocabularies. Words can be housed in small file boxes, hole-punched and placed on curtain rings, or kept in notebooks.

• Have students select three words that they have found in material read or heard. Have them design a lesson that uses at least one of the 20 brain-compatible strategies and take turns teaching one of their words to the class. The class may select several of the words to include in their individual word banks or on the word wall.

Reciprocal Teaching and Cooperative Learning

• Have students read and reread books that introduce new content-area vocabulary words aloud to a partner. As more words are encountered, more words are mastered.

• Have students quiz one another on the definitions of key vocabulary words.

Role Plays, Drama, Pantomimes, and Charades

• Have students role play, or act out, vocabulary words. By playing Charades, one student is selected to act out or dramatize the meaning of a word. The class attempts to guess the word. This can be turned into a game by awarding points to the first student or the first team to guess the designated word. For example, for the word *exhausted,* a student could come to the front of the class and act as if (s)he is too tired to do anything.

• The strategy of role play is particularly great for helping students understand both the literal and the figurative meaning of words, such as idioms. Select a student to come to the front of the room and give that student a card containing an idiom or other type of figurative language statement, such as *You've got me hanging on a string.* The student then dramatizes both the literal and figurative meaning of the statement.

Storytelling

• Have students work together in cooperative groups to develop language experience stories that incorporate vocabulary words they are trying to learn. The stories must contain all of the designated words used in the appropriate context. Encourage students to create the wildest, weirdest, or funniest story they can. The wilder, the more memorable!

• When teaching figurative language, literature like the following as read-alouds and place them in the classroom for student enjoyment:

The King Who Rained, by Fred Gwynne

A Little Pigeon Toad, by Fred Gwynne

2107 Curious Word Origins, by Charles Funk

The Amelia Bedelia Series, by Beverly Cleary

Visualization

• Have students visualize the spelling of a vocabulary word as they write the word in the air.

• Create a visualization that links a vocabulary word with its meaning. For example, when teaching the word *scullery,* have students visualize a black and white tile kitchen floor with a stark, white skull lying in the middle. The visualization practically ensures that students will recall a scullery room as a room adjacent to a kitchen.

Visuals

• Write vocabulary words on the board, chart paper, or an overhead as you teach the words so that students can see them in print.

• Color-code key vocabulary words by writing them in blue on a dry-erase board or chart paper. Blue is an appealing color to the brain. Words that you wish to emphasize should be written in red, orange, or another high-energy color.

• Have students remember key vocabulary words or concepts in their notes by color-coding them using color markers, crayons, or colored pencils.

• Place key vocabulary words on the wall categorized by the letters of the alphabet. Continue to add to the *Word Wall* throughout the year.

• Have students survey content-area texts and look for visual indicators of key vocabulary words such as words in boldface print or words in italics. Teach them that these words are highlighted for a reason, probably because they are integral to comprehension of the chapter or unit.

Writing and Journals

• Before the reading of expository or narrative text, have students write their own original definition of a key vocabulary word. As instruction proceeds, students can compare their original definitions with the actual ones.

• Following instruction, have students write the definitions of key vocabulary words in their own words.

• Have students write original stories containing the vocabulary words to be learned. The more ludicrous the story, the more memorable for the brain.

• Identify simple vocabulary words that are overused in students' writing, such as *a lot*, *like*, *good*, or *saw*. Have students brainstorm a list of words that mean the same thing as the *tired word*. These synonyms will enlarge students' writing vocabularies and give students other options for making their writing more interesting. For example, for the word *good*, the list of brainstormed words could include *marvelous*, *superb*, *exquisite*, and *phenomenal*. Students are not allowed to use the overused words but must incorporate the appropriate synonyms into their writing vocabularies.

REFLECTION AND APPLICATION

> ## Which strategies can I use to teach vocabulary so that my students' brains are engaged?

Standard/Objective: _____

_____

_____.

Activity: _____

_____

_____.

Standard/Objective: _____

_____

_____.

Activity: _____

_____

_____.

Standard/Objective: _____

_____

_____.

Activity: _____

_____

_____.

Standard/Objective: _____

_____

_____.

Activity: _____

_____

_____.

Standard/Objective: _____

_____

_____.

Activity: _____

_____

_____.

5

Text Comprehension Instruction

Reading = D × C

Reading = Decoding × Comprehension

—Phil Gough, Reading Researcher

Have you ever heard someone say, "I read that passage but I don't remember a thing I read"? Without understanding and memory, has any true reading actually taken place?

Prior to the 1970s, reading comprehension was viewed as more of a passive than an active process. Teachers were spending little time on direct instruction in this area. According to Delores Durkin's observational studies (1979), of the 4,469 minutes of observed reading instruction in fourth grade, only 20 minutes were spent in direct comprehension instruction. In 2004, Wolfe and Nevills defined comprehension as the active "process of attaching meaning to written or spoken language by accessing previously stored experience or knowledge" (p. 156).

In the late 1970s, theorists began researching comprehension strategies that could be taught and would actually assist students in understanding text. More than 30 years of research provide evidence to support the efficacy of strategy instruction in the area of reading comprehension. The National Reading Panel delineates the following six such strategies: comprehension monitoring, graphic and semantic organizers, question answering, question generating, story structure, and summarizing. Each comprehension strategy is described in the paragraphs that follow.

Good readers realize when they comprehend what they are reading and when they do not. They will often stop and reread a passage for understanding. Instructing students in comprehension monitoring therefore encourages them to realize what they actually understand, identify what they do not really understand, and use the appropriate strategies to correct problems in comprehension (Partnership for Reading, 2001).

Graphic organizers, also referred to as semantic, mind, and concept maps, benefit both left and right hemispheres of the brain because they are pictorial representations of linear ideas. Graphic organizers are particularly helpful in assisting students when reading expository text from content areas. They can also be used with narrative text or stories. Word webs are essential for increasing vocabulary recognition because they can connect a key word to its synonyms and antonyms.

Teacher questioning is crucial if students are to get the most out of their reading and is most effective when the questions do the following: (1) set a purpose or reason to read, (2) assist students in focusing attention on what they should be learning, (3) help students to engage the brain actively in reading, (4) motivate students to monitor their understanding, and (5) provide students with opportunities to connect what they are learning to what they already know (Partnership for Reading, 2001).

The number one purpose of the brain is survival. Formulating one's own questions regarding real-life situations enables students to use the brain for the reason it exists in the first place. Therefore, having students generate original questions and answer them is a natural process that facilitates comprehension and actively engages the student with the text.

Students who realize the structure of stories experience increased appreciation, comprehension, and memory (Partnership for Reading, 2001). Students can be taught to identify the elements of a story's plot including the setting, character traits, goals, attempts, and outcomes. One type of graphic organizer, a story map, shows the events of the plot in sequential order.

One of the most difficult strategies for students is summarizing. Summarizing includes taking the most crucial ideas in a text, condensing them, and putting them into the student's own words. This skill enables students to recognize the major ideas, connect those ideas to the central theme of the text, eliminate unnecessary text, and retain what is read (Partnership for Reading, 2001).

RELEVANT RESEARCH

The following seven strategies, when utilized, characterize a highly effective reader: the ability to (1) activate prior knowledge; (2) infer, or *read the author's mind*; (3) monitor what is being read and clarify what may be confusing; (4) generate and answer questions; (5) search for and select the appropriate information needed; (6) summarize or restate ideas from the text in one's own words; and (7) visualize and organize what has been read through the use of personally constructed graphic organizers (McEwan, 2004, p. 35).

Readers ask purposeful questions before, during, and after reading (Miller, 2002).

Good readers know that the most interesting questions are not those addressed explicitly in the text but those interpreted by the reader (Miller, 2002).

Hearing other students' questions and listening to other students' answers inspires new questions and new answers in each student (Miller, 2002).

Successful secondary readers have the ability to utilize questions to discern the most important information in text and to clarify those points that might cause confusion (Strong, Silver, Perini, & Tuculescu, 2002).

Successful secondary readers realize when they are confused or mistaken in their understanding of texts and are capable of using appropriate strategies to fix their comprehension (Strong et al., 2002).

Collaborative summarizing assists students in building their independence and confidence in creating effective summaries (Silver, Strong, & Perini, 2001).

When students come up with their own questions before, during, and after reading, comprehension is increased (McEwan, 2001).

Students need to be taught the "look back" strategy, which shows them how to go back to the text they have already read to look for answers to specific questions (McEwan, 2001).

Good readers read with a purpose in mind, whether that purpose is gathering information, meeting course requirements, or entertaining oneself (Partnership for Reading, 2001).

Good readers use their personal experiences as well as their knowledge of the world, vocabulary, language, and reading strategies to make meaning out of text (Partnership for Reading, 2001).

Comprehension for text is increased when readers are taught to use specific comprehension strategies (Partnership for Reading, 2001).

Through the steps of explicit instruction, modeling, guided practice, and application, teachers can demonstrate to students which comprehension strategies to use, why and when they should use them, and how to apply them to the text (Partnership for Reading, 2001).

It is more realistic for students to generate their own questions because that is what people are required to do in real life (Sternberg & Grigorenko, 2000).

Having students organize their thoughts and ideas while reading into a visual graph assists students in recalling what they have read and may transfer to improved achievement in the content areas of science and social studies (National Reading Panel, 2000).

Having students generate their own questions appears to increase comprehension best when this strategy is part of an instructional program that incorporates many strategies (National Reading Panel, 2000).

The skill of summarizing is useful for teaching students to identify main ideas, omit details, integrate ideas, and make generalizations (National Reading Panel, 2000).

A comprehension strategy framework encompasses the following three interactive phases: (1) prereading, which includes determining prior knowledge, building students' background and relating it to their prior knowledge, and concentrating on the comprehension strategy to be taught; (2) active reading, which includes setting a purpose, reading silently, monitoring; and (3) active discussion, which helps students feel a part of the story they have read (Dowhower, 1999).

Graphic organizers enable students to see how bits of information are connected, make that information easier to recall, and provide opportunities for students to break information into meaningful segments (Parry & Gregory, 1998).

When readers are proficient, they know what they are (or are not) comprehending and when they are (or are not) comprehending (Keene & Zimmermann, 1997).

Students develop and use comprehension strategies best while actively engaged in reading and the discussion that follows (Clay, 1991; Fountas & Pinnell, 1996).

Seventy-seven percent of students who took arts-enriched classes scored at grade level on standardized reading tests, compared with 55% at grade level for the control group (Gardiner, 1996).

Mapping helps students understand verbal, nonverbal, concrete, or abstract concepts because maps integrate both the visual and the verbal (Sousa, 1995).

Ten years of research indicate that comprehension for elementary students is facilitated when graphic organizers are constructed prior to reading; vocabulary and comprehension scores are improved for secondary students when graphic organizers are constructed after reading (Dunston, 1992).

STRATEGIC ACTIVITIES

Objective: Monitor comprehension when reading narrative and expository texts

Brainstorming and Discussion

• Schedule individual conferences to find out what strategies students are using when they come to a part of the text they do not understand. As they are reading along and come to a part of the text that may be confusing, such as a vocabulary word they do not know, ask the students what should be done to figure out the meaning of the unknown word. Students should use one or more of the following techniques: *Reread the passage to see if I can figure it out* or *Skip the word and read on to see if I can go back and figure it out.*

• Ask the following questions in support of the student's use of self-monitoring behaviors:

Were you correct?

Where's the word that gave you trouble (following an error)?

What's wrong?

Why did you stop reading?

What letter would you expect to be at the beginning of the word?

What letter would you expect to be at the end of the word?

Would the word _____ make sense here?

What do you think it looks like?

It could possibly be _____, but consider _____.

Does is look right and sound right to you?

SOURCE: Adapted from Clay, 1993; Goodman, 1996; Routman, 1991; Department of Education [New Zealand], 1985.

Manipulatives

• As students read independently, have them place a Post-It note on any part of the story they do not understand. Use informal observation to ascertain where most of the confusion may be. Engage students in a class discussion of the parts that appear to be the most confusing.

Reciprocal Teaching and Cooperative Learning

• Have students read selected text aloud to a partner. When one student does not comprehend a part of the text, the partner helps to explain those passages in question.

• Have each student select a close partner or a student sitting so close that the student can talk with this person and does not need to get out of his or her seat. As students read narrative or content-area texts, have them turn to their close partners and answer questions or explain in their own words a concept that the teacher has just taught.

• Divide students into groups, with the number of students in each group equal to the sections there are to be studied. Each student in a group reads and studies a different portion of a story, chapter, or unit of study. Each student then teaches what he or she has learned to the remaining members of the group and quizzes group members until convinced that everyone knows his or her part thoroughly enough to pass a test on the content. This activity is called *jigsaw* because each student is responsible for a piece of the puzzle (Johnson, Johnson, & Holubeck, 1990).

• Have students work in pairs and interview one another regarding a book that each student has read. Students then give an oral report to the class on their partner's book (Tate, 2003).

• Have students work in small cooperative groups to write a play or a Reader's Theater together. The group practices and then performs the play for the entire class (Tate, 2003).

Objective: Use or design graphic organizers to comprehend narrative and expository text

 ### Graphic Organizers, Semantic Maps, and Word Webs

• Have students use the following graphic organizer to show that the supporting details in a passage or story should add up to the main idea.

Main Idea/Details

Details

┌─────────────────────────────┐
│   │
└─────────────────────────────┘

┌─────────────────────────────┐
│   │
└─────────────────────────────┘

┌─────────────────────────────┐
│   │
└─────────────────────────────┘

+ ┌─────────────────────────────┐
       │   │
       └─────────────────────────────┘

─────────────────────────────────────

Main Idea ┌─────────────────────────────┐
               │   │
               └─────────────────────────────┘

• Have students use the following graphic organizer to show that every action results in an effect.

Cause / Effect

So

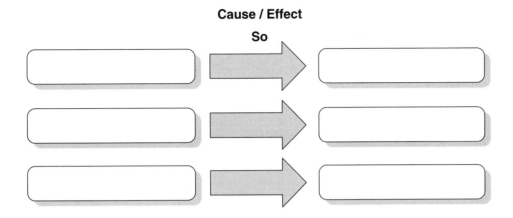

- Have students use the following graphic organizer to show a character's or historical figure's traits and delineate evidence in support of those traits.

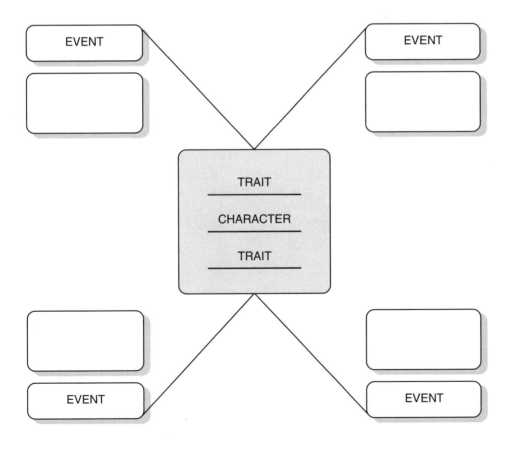

- Have students use the following graphic organizer to show the sequential order of events in narrative or expository texts.

Sequence

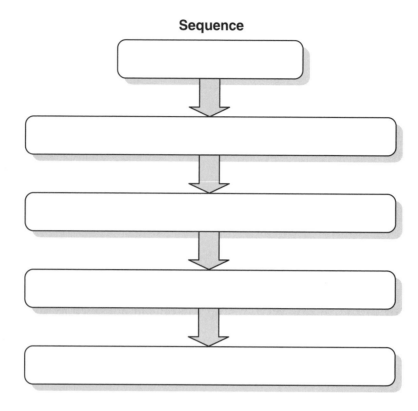

• Have students use the following graphic organizer, called a Venn diagram, to compare and contrast two parallel concepts. For example, following the reading of two history chapters, students could compare and contrast the Civil War with the Revolutionary War.

Compare / Contrast

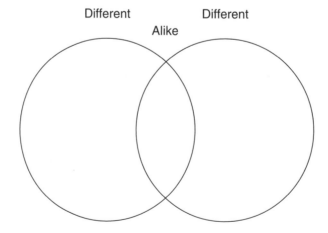

• Have students use the following graphic organizer to list the major problems in either a narrative or an expository text and possible solutions to those problems.

Problem   **Solution**

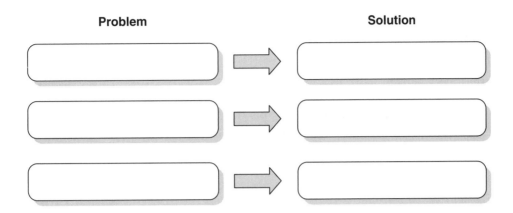

- Have students use the following fishbone graphic organizer to break down a concept into its critical attributes or show cause and effect.

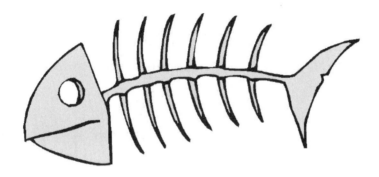

- Have students complete a semantic, concept, or mind map to show the relationships between story events or major concepts. Encourage students to construct their own original mind maps as they become familiar with this type of graphic organizer.

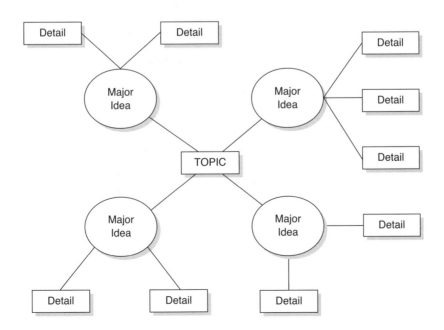

Objective: Answer questions
regarding narrative and expository text

 Brainstorming and Discussion

• Have students answer questions from narrative or content-area text at all six levels of Bloom's taxonomy. Use the following question stems as guides:

Knowledge Level

Who, What, When, Where, How, How Much

Choose, Which Is the Best One

Comprehension Level

State in Your Own Words

What Does This Mean

Indicate, Explain, Translate

Application Level

Predict What Would Happen If

Identify the Results of

Tell What Would Happen If

Analysis Level

What Conclusions

State the Point of View of

What Is the Theme, Main Idea

What Can We Conclude

Synthesis Level

Create

Make, Do

Design, Compose, Develop

Evaluation Level

Judge, Appraise

Criticize, Defend

Find the Errors

Field Trips

- Prior to taking students on a field trip, have them assist in generating a list of questions covering the major points to be answered from the trip. The questions give the class a purpose for taking the trip. Students will ask and answer the questions both during and following the trip.

- Before taking students on a field trip, visit the site of the trip and create a scavenger hunt with questions to which students should find the answers while on the trip. Students can have fun finding all of the answers while on the field trip.

Games

- Create a list of questions regarding a story or content-area text. Have students work in cooperative groups to be the first group to locate the answers to all of the questions on the list.

Graphic Organizers, Semantic Maps, and Word Webs

- While studying a content area, have small groups of students generate original questions to place at the center of a question web. A question web is a graphic organizer with a question at its center. Students then read related material (picture books, books, magazines, information gleaned from the Internet) and place possible information to answer the question on the question web. A sample follows:

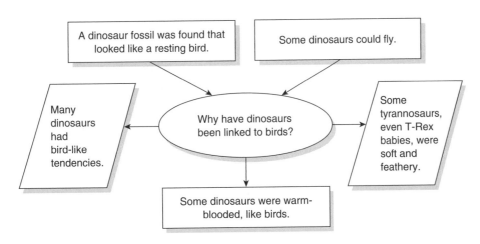

Metaphors, Analogies, and Similes

- Have students learn to answer main idea questions by comparing the concept to a table using the following simile: Tell students that a main idea is similar to the top of the table while the details in a story or content-area text are similar to the legs. Just like the top of the table cannot stand without the legs, a main idea cannot stand without support from the details. Have students draw a table with four legs. Read a story or content-area text and have students write the main idea on the top of the table and one of the details that supports the main idea on each leg of the table (Tate, 2003).

Movement

• Have students answer cause-and-effect questions by forming a cause-effect chain. Have students stand and form a circle. Join the circle and begin by stating a cause such as *I had to stay in my room all day.* The next person in the circle to the left repeats the cause and gives an effect that follows the stated cause such as, *I had to stay in my room all day, so I could not go outside and play.* The next person to the left continues the chain by stating, *I could not go outside and play, so I began to cry.* The cause-effect chain continues. Following this activity, remind students that words such as *so* and *because* signal cause-and-effect relationships.

• Have students learn to put events in sequential order. Following the reading of a story, list its important events on separate cards. Give out the cards randomly to students in class. Have students with cards get up and arrange themselves in order by reading the cards of other classmates and arranging themselves in sequential order according to the story's events. Have each student read the event on his or her card aloud to the class. Have other students in the class tell whether the students with cards are standing in correct order. If an event is out of sequence, students should determine the appropriate place for it, and the student moves to the place.

Music, Rhythm, Rhyme, and Rap

• Select a song with lyrics that are appropriate for your students' age and grade level. Play the song and have students listen and enjoy. Then give students a list of questions to be answered from the song lyrics. Play the song a second time and have students listen for the answers in the lyrics.

Project-Based and Problem-Based Instruction

• Give students a real-life project to complete or problem to solve. Have them answer a list of questions in an effort to complete the project or solve the problem.

Objective: Generate Questions regarding narrative and expository text

Brainstorming and Discussion

• Before, during, and after the reading of narrative or content-area text, assist students in linking their background experiences and schema to the text by asking some of the following questions: *What do you already know about _____? How does that relate to your life? Has that ever happened to you?*

- Share one of your favorite pieces of literature with your class. Discuss how the text of the book or poem raised questions for you so that your students know that even the best readers have questions regarding the text. For example, a question I raised regarding one of my favorite novels is *Why did Maya Angelou name her book* I Know Why the Caged Bird Sings, *and what did that title have to do with the theme of the book?*

- Have students formulate questions at all six levels of Bloom's taxonomy regarding narrative or content-area text. Have students use the question stems provided earlier in this section.

- When reading content-area texts, have students turn bold headings and subheadings into questions and then read for the purpose of answering the formulated questions. For example, the heading *Causes of the Civil War* could be turned into *Name three causes of the Civil War* or *What are three causes of the Civil War?*

- Teach students the SQ3R technique for generating and answering questions regarding content-area text. The steps in the SQ3R technique are as follows:

    Survey. Students preview a chapter in a content-area textbook. They look at bold headings, captions, illustrations, italicized or boldface vocabulary words, and so on.

    Question. Students formulate and write down questions that they would like to have answered based on the information gleaned during the preview. They turn headings into questions.

    Read. Students read for the express purpose of answering the questions generated during the previous question stage of the technique. They write the answers to the questions in their own words rather than copying them from the text.

    Recite. Students read each question and tell the answer in their own words.

    Review. Students review the questions and answers after a 24-hour period and then periodically to facilitate memory.

- Students use Stauffer's (1975) *Directed Reading-Thinking Activity (DR-TA)* with both narrative and content-area text by predicting from a picture or the title of a story or chapter what the text will be about and then reading a segment of the text to confirm those predictions. Students then make another prediction from the new text read. The sequence of predicting, validating, and predicting again continues until the end of the text.

Field Trips

- Before a scheduled field trip, students generate questions that they would like to have answered during the trip. Students bring the questions with them and attempt to find answers either from observations or asking authority figures on the trip. Following the trip, the answers to selected questions are discussed.

Games

• Students play *Who Am I?* by selecting a historical figure or book character who has been studied in class. One student is selected to stand before the class and take on the persona of the figure or character. Other students try to guess the name of the figure or character by generating questions that can be answered with *yes* or *no*. The first student to guess the correct name of the figure is the winner.

• Construct a *Jeopardy!* game board by selecting the most important concepts in a designated content-area chapter. These main points form the answers and are placed on a game board in categories of 100, 200, 300, 400, and 500 points. The simplest answers are worth 100 points and the most difficult worth 500 points. Post-It notes on chart paper or a board work well as the *Jeopardy!* game board. Students are placed on teams with members of varying abilities and take turns generating the questions for the designated answers. The game follows the rules for the television show *Jeopardy!*

Graphic Organizers, Semantic Maps, and Word Webs

• Before reading either expository or a narrative text, have students complete the following graphic organizer (showing the KNL Strategy) indicating what they already *Know* about the topic (prior knowledge), what they *Need* to know about it (purpose of the reading), and, after reading, what they *Learned*.

The K-N-L Strategy		
Topic:		
_____		
_____		
What I Know	*What I Need to Know*	*What I Learned*

Humor

• Have students work individually or with a partner to create riddles that demonstrate their knowledge of content-area text. For example, after a study of the pilgrims and the first Thanksgiving, students could create the riddle, "What flower does not grow in the ground?" Answer: The Mayflower.

Music

• Ask several students to bring in a CD containing one of their favorite songs. Allow students to listen to each other's favorites. (Be certain the lyrics of the song are screened in advance for inappropriate language.) After the class listens to a song, have students generate questions to ask other students about the lyrics they have just heard. Students take turns coming to the front of the class and reading one of their questions aloud. The other members of the class provide answers to the questions read.

Reciprocal Teaching and Cooperative Learning

• Following the introduction to a story, have students work in pairs or small groups to write questions they would like to have answered before reading the entire text.

• Following the preview of a content-area chapter or unit of study, have students work in pairs or small groups to write questions they would like to have answered before reading of the entire chapter or unit.

Writing and Journals

• Have students read narrative or content-area texts for the purpose of answering questions that they generated. Students should write the answers to at least five student-generated questions.

• Have students work together to formulate test questions for an exam. Questions should be based on the most significant understanding from the course content.

Objective: Use story structure to comprehend narrative text

Brainstorming and Discussion

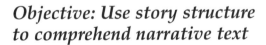

• To understand story structure, have students discuss answers to the following five questions (National Reading Panel, 2000):

1. Who is the main character?
2. Where and when did the story take place?
3. What did the main characters do?
4. How did the story end?
5. How did the main character feel?

Graphic Organizers, Semantic Maps, and Word Webs

• Have students complete the following story map to demonstrate their understanding of the structure of a story heard or read.

Story Map

Title: _____

Setting:

```
┌────────────────────────────┐
│                            │
│                            │
│                            │
└────────────────────────────┘
```

Characters: _____   _____

_____   _____

_____   _____

Problem:

```
┌────────────────────────────┐
│                            │
│                            │
│                            │
└────────────────────────────┘
```

Event 1: _____

Event 2: _____

Event 3: _____

Event 4: _____

Solution:

```
┌────────────────────────────┐
│                            │
│                            │
│                            │
└────────────────────────────┘
```

• After practice with completing graphic organizers, have students construct their own story map regarding a story of choice. Story maps can include but are not limited to the following: main characters, setting, problem, significant events, and solution.

Movement

• Delineate the main sequential events in a story and write each main event on a separate card. Give out the cards randomly to students. Have students with cards come to the front of the room and arrange themselves in the order in which the events in the story occurred.

Reciprocal Teaching and Cooperative Learning

• Have students retell a story to a partner. This story should be one previously told or read to the class. Have students include the main characters, the setting, problem, significant events, and solution.

Storytelling

• Read a story aloud for enjoyment. During a rereading of the same story, have students identify the main character, setting, actions of the main characters, story conclusion, and the characters' feelings.

Objective: Summarize narrative and expository text

Brainstorming and Discussion

• Following the reading of a content-area passage or story, demonstrate to students the thought processes involved when one summarizes. Assist them in determining which ideas are important enough to be part of the summary and which ideas are less significant. Then read several prepared summaries so that students can perceive what an appropriate summary would sound like.

Metaphors, Analogies, and Similes

• Tell students that a summary is like a text message on a cell phone. Explain that only the most important words are included in both. Have students read a passage and then write a summary as if it is a text message.

Reciprocal Teaching and Cooperative Learning

• Explain to students that a summary consists of only a few sentences that give the main idea of a chapter, story, book, movie, and so on. Tell them that summaries restate in one's own words the meaning or "gist" of what was heard or read. Show students several examples of good summaries, such as an obituary from the paper as a summary of someone's life. Have students work with a partner to write a summary of the most important events in their lives to this point. Eventually, have students begin to write summaries by selecting the most important ideas in a story or in content-area text.

- Have students use the following checklist to evaluate their partner's summary of content-area text:

_____ Does the summary tell the main idea of the text?

_____ Is the main idea the first thing stated?

_____ Does the summary include all of the most important ideas?

_____ Does the summary include only the most important ideas?

_____ Is the summary brief and concise?

_____ Is the summary clear to the reader?

SOURCE: Adapted from Gunning, 1996, p. 213.

- During a cooperative learning activity, appoint a student to be the summarizer. The job of the summarizer is periodically to stop the group's discussion of the assigned topic and provide an oral summary of the major points that group members have made to this point.

Writing and Journals

- Use a cloze technique similar to the one that follows to help students with summarizing. After reading a passage on the brain, students could complete the following summary paragraph.

There are four major ways to gain students' attention during an instructional lesson. The first way is _____. Need is defined as _____. The second way is _____. Novelty is defined as _____. The third way is _____. Meaning is defined as _____. Finally, the fourth major way is _____. Emotion is defined as _____.

REFLECTION AND APPLICATION

> ### Which strategies can I use
> ### to teach text comprehension so
> ### that my students' brains are engaged?

Standard/Objective: _____

_____

_____.

Activity: _____

_____

_____.

Standard/Objective: _____

_____

_____.

Activity: _____

_____

_____.

Standard/Objective: _____

_____

_____.

Activity: _____

_____

_____.

Standard/Objective: _____

_____

_____.

Activity: _____

_____

_____.

Standard/Objective: _____

_____

_____.

Activity: _____

_____

_____.

PART II
Language Arts Strategies

6

Reading Authentically

Reading is a basic competency required for success in the real world of work.

—Secretary's Commission on
Achieving Necessary Skills, 1991

One thing that neuroscientific research tells us is that purpose is crucially important to the brain. We realize that people live longer when in pursuit of life's purpose. We know that people who retire after a long career need to stay active with new purposes or they don't live very long after they retire. We know that many teenagers who have no short- or long-term goals (in other words, no positive purpose) flounder and often find themselves involved with gangs or drugs.

A reader's comprehension is also improved when the brain is engaged in text with a specific purpose in mind. Sometimes that purpose is for the acquisition of new information. Other times it is to complete a task that living in the real world requires, such as studying the driver's manual for the purpose of passing the test or reading an instruction manual in an effort to assemble a newly-purchased item. The SCANS (Secretary's Commission on Achieving Necessary Skills) Report (1991) lists reading as one of the basic skills necessary for success in the real world of employment. At other times, a reader's purpose is self-help or sheer pleasure—to be swept up in the lives of real or imagined characters brought to life in the creative mind of a skilled craftsperson.

Whatever the purpose of reading, students should be consistently marinated in a variety of both print and nonprint material to ensure that the skill of reading is lifelong.

RELEVANT RESEARCH

Students read from a wide range of print and nonprint texts to build an understanding of texts, of themselves, and of the cultures of the United States and the world to acquire new information; to respond to the needs and demands of society and the workplace; and for personal fulfillment. Among these texts are fiction, nonfiction, classic, and contemporary works (National Council of Teachers of English/ International Reading Association, 1996, Standard I).

Students get little experience in interpreting the structure in nonfiction texts, making comprehension difficult (Strong et al., 2002).

Students should be making constant connections between the text and themselves (text-to-self), one text and another text (text-to-text), and the text and the world at large (text-to-world) (Miller, 2002).

When students understand the structure of texts, they can use graphic organizers that follow that structure to list crucial information from the text (Strong et al., 2002).

Students have difficulty seeing the organizational patterns in nonfiction texts because they have little exposure to this structure in the elementary grades (Strong et al., 2002).

Content-area picture books and those with short text allow students to discuss events of historical significance and build background knowledge (Harvey & Goudvis, 2000).

Students in Grades 4, 8, and 12, who were engaged in more reading on a daily basis, both at school and at home, had higher scores than peers less engaged in reading (National Center for Education Statistics, 1999).

Agendas, notes from lectures, units of study, and important characteristics of major concepts can be represented by mind maps that students can construct either individually or in cooperative groups (Parry & Gregory, 1998).

Mindscapes, mapping, and graphic organizers enrich learning because the brain thinks both linearly and randomly (Jensen, 1997).

The SCANS Report lists reading and writing as two of the basic competencies required for success in the real world of work (SCANS, 1991).

The level of literacy that U.S. citizens need to possess is constantly increasing. Many wire service articles are written at an 11th-grade level and sports pages at the ninth- or tenth-grade level (Fiske, 1983).

STRATEGIC ACTIVITIES

Objective: Read authentically to understand self, society, and the world

Brainstorming and Discussion

- Have students read nonfiction texts that exemplify the problem and solution text structure. For example, select a timely topic that represents a societal problem, such as rising gas prices. Have students read a newspaper or magazine article related to the topic. Have them use the problem-solution text structure (found in Chapter 8) to brainstorm possible answers to the problem, such as car pooling, driving fuel-efficient vehicles, and so on.

- Introduce students to the following statements: *history repeats itself, what goes around comes around; people who do not learn from their mistakes are doomed to repeat them.* Have students discuss the meaning inherent in these sayings and lead them to examples in U.S. history that demonstrate these concepts. Use the cycle structure for nonfiction texts (found in Chapter 8) and a cycle graphic organizer to assist students in comprehending this text structure.

Drawing and Artwork

- Have students describe and illustrate the step-by-step procedures to an everyday task, such as brushing one's teeth or starting a car, or for assembling an everyday item. This will help improve their ability to write clearly and descriptively. Students can then exchange their descriptions and illustrations with one another and follow the steps prescribed to ascertain whether the directions are clear enough for the task to be completed.

Games

- Acquaint students with the major parts of the daily newspaper. Have them work in cooperative groups to participate in a scavenger hunt. Give each group a list of 20–25 questions that can be answered quickly by reading selected parts of the paper, such as *What is the name of one movie playing at the Starlight Cinema?* or *What was the average rainfall over the last two days?* Groups compete to be the first to find all of the correct answers on the sheet.

Graphic Organizers, Semantic Maps, and Word Webs

- Have students develop a timeline that represents the logical order of a sequence of events. To help them understand the concept, have them construct a timeline of their lives from birth to their current age. Have students place the significant life events on the timeline in the appropriate chronological order. Then ask students to apply the timeline concept to significant events in U.S. or world history.

- Have students use the Venn diagram and the sequence of events, problem and solution, and cause-effect graphic organizers contained in the graphic organizer section of Chapter 5 to assist them in understanding both fiction and nonfiction texts.

Humor

- Have students find editorial cartoons in the newspaper and bring them to class. Ask them to share their cartoons with a cooperative group that can assist them in determining the deeper meaning inherent in this type of genre. Have the group discuss how the cartoon reflects societal issues and what message it is attempting to convey. As students improve in their inferential thinking, have them interpret these cartoons for themselves, independent of the group.

Music, Rhythm, Rhyme, and Rap

- Have students listen to the music of different eras in U.S. history. Have them discuss the events that were occurring during that era and ways in which those events influenced the music that was written and performed. For example, during the Vietnam War era, songs such as "Blowing in the Wind" by Peter, Paul and Mary and "The Windows of the World" written by Burt Bacharach and performed by Dionne Warwick reflected the antiwar sentiment that some people felt during those times.

Reciprocal Teaching and Cooperative Learning

- Have students work with a partner to survey and interpret the charts and graphs connected to a unit of study in a content-area text or contained in a daily newspaper. Give students a list of questions related to the selected charts or graphs and have them work together to find the answers in as little time as possible.

Storytelling

- Have students select both fiction and nonfiction books from a given list of classic or contemporary works. Each student's assignment is to read a chosen book and then create a way to tell the story of its content to the class, such as designing a book jacket that depicts the main idea.

- Refer to the extensive list of *Great Books for Teaching Content in History, Social Studies, Science, Music, Art, and Literacy* found in Appendix B of the text *Strategies That Work* by Harvey and Goudvis (2000). The sub-headings *World Exploration, U.S. History, World History, General History Series* and *Social Studies* provide teachers with annotated selections for assisting students in understanding themselves and the world.

Work Study and Apprenticeships

• Have students use their reading and language arts skills to fulfill job requirements for a practicum, internship, or any other task where literacy skills are integrated into authentic job-related tasks; for example, completing a job application or following the instructions of a job manual.

Writing and Journals

• Have students respond to societal needs and demands by successfully completing a necessary everyday task such as writing a check or reading the driver's manual in preparation to take and pass the driver's test.

• Provide time each day for students to write in a diary or journal regarding incidents that are personally important. Personal journals are not typically graded but allow students opportunities to hone their writing craft as they describe incidents that happened at home, reflect on personal class assignments, or express feelings and emotions related to an event.

REFLECTION AND APPLICATION

> Which strategies can I use to engage
> students' brains so that they read authentically?

Standard/Objective: _____

_____

_____.

Activity: _____

_____

_____.

Standard/Objective: _____

_____

_____.

Activity: _____

_____

_____.

Standard/Objective: _____

_____

_____.

Activity: _____

_____

_____.

Standard/Objective: _____

_____

_____.

Activity: _____

_____

_____.

Standard/Objective: _____

_____

_____.

Activity: _____

_____

_____.

7

Reading Widely

Rooms that are filled with a variety of printed materials have students who find reading contagious.

—Harvey & Goudvis, 2000

It has been said that we learn to do by doing. Michael Jordan became an exceptional basketball player by engaging in an inordinate amount of practice at shooting baskets. Tiger Woods became an extraordinary golfer by putting in countless hours practicing his craft on the golf course. Wouldn't it stand to reason that a student learns to read by practicing the act of reading itself? Yet many students would rather do anything but read. Research even tells us that the very students who need to engage in the act of real reading are most often the ones spending time in the artificial act of completing worksheets. Why is this the case?

In this decade, teachers must face the fact that they are teaching students with brains unlike any in the history of the world. They are teaching students who are used to the rapidly changing input of the video game and the computer. They are teaching students who are not accustomed to visualizing scenes in stories, as good readers do, because the toys with which they play display everything in technicolor and cinemascope. To these brains, visualization is unnecessary. All is not lost, however. Teachers who are passionate about good literature and who provide students with real-life opportunities to read widely have students who are passionate about literature and who realize the value of a lifelong love of literacy. For example, my daughter Jessica had a reading and language arts teacher in the sixth grade who loved Edgar Alan Poe. It wasn't long before Jessica was reading everything that Poe had ever written.

RELEVANT RESEARCH

Students read a wide range of literature from many periods in many genres to build an understanding of the many dimensions (e.g., philosophical, ethical, aesthetic) of human experience (NCTE/IRA, 1996, Standard II).

In every classroom, students should have access to a multitude of genres including the following: historical and realistic fiction, autobiographies and biographies, folktales and tall tales, diaries, fantasy and fables, memoirs, poetry, and expository texts (Anderson, 2004).

Every classroom library should consist of more than 300 titles that are age appropriate, are of high interest, and represent a variety of formats and genres including magazines, short articles, and books to entice struggling readers (Anderson, 2004).

A strong correlation exists between growth in the reading achievement of second- through fifth-graders and the time they spend engaged in reading real books (Anderson, Wilson, & Fielding, 1988).

Because of the recent popularity of nonfiction trade books, it is possible to teach any genre topic with picture books and nonfiction trade books (Harvey & Goudvis, 2000).

When instruction is centered around a variety of genres, students become familiar with the unique characteristics and conventions of nonfiction, fiction, poetry, and so forth (Harvey & Goudvis, 2000).

Rooms that are filled with a variety of printed materials have students who find reading contagious (Harvey & Goudvis, 2000).

If teachers do not offer primary students multiple experiences with informational texts, they are adding to future difficulties that students will have reading these types of texts, which contributes to the slump in fourth-grade reading scores (Yopp & Yopp, 2000).

Collaborative Strategic Reading (CSR) promotes reading comprehension, content learning, and the acquisition of English by combining two instructional approaches—reading comprehension instruction and cooperative learning (Klingner & Vaughn, 1999).

Authorship does not begin when the student struggles to put something into print; it commences with a sense of awareness about life. *Writing does not begin with deskwork but with lifework* (Calkins, 1994, p. 3).

STRATEGIC ACTIVITIES

Objective: Read widely in an effort to understand dimensions of human experience

Brainstorming and Discussion

• Define the term *genre* for students as *a specific type of literature*. Have students brainstorm the various genres that they can name. List their brainstormed ideas on the board. Add to students' list any major genre they may have omitted. Explain that literate citizens read a variety of genres and that this class will be doing the same.

Music, Rhythm, Rhyme, and Rap

- Locate and bring to class music representative of a number of periods of history. Have students discuss the events that may have influenced the music of each period. Have students read literary selections that characterize the designated periods.

Project-Based and Problem-Based Instruction

- Have students experience a wide variety of literature by reading around the following genre wheel. Students may start at any place on the wheel but must read one or more selections from each genre. Have students find creative ways to report on at least five of the many books read. You may provide students with a list of literary selections from which they can choose a variety of genres.

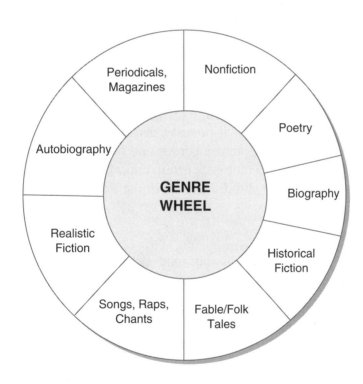

- Classroom libraries enable students to read a variety of books that have aesthetic, philosophical, and ethnic appeal. Consult the annotated bibliography of books appropriate for both junior and senior high school levels found in the text *Reading Reasons* by Kelly Gallagher. This list is found in Appendix B: 101 Books Every Classroom Library Should Have.

- In an effort to entice students into the act of reading, display classroom library books in the following ways:

1. On a clothesline hung with clothespins slightly above students' heads

2. In inexpensive plastic rain gutters bought at a hardware store and affixed to the walls of the classroom

3. Five or six books laid out on chalk trays to be used in book talks

4. On each student's desk before class. Have students spend a few minutes reading the book on their desks and then passing it on to other students (Gallagher, 2003)

• A social studies or history class is the perfect opportunity for students to experience a variety of literature from varying periods in history. Have students read historical fiction books about characters who lived during a particular period or autobiographies and biographies about people who played major roles in history. Integrating this literature into actual history units is one of the best ways to make the literature meaningful.

• Have students find articles from the newspaper, a magazine, or the Internet related to a particular topic they are studying. Have them read each article and then list the five most important points to share with a classmate.

Reciprocal Teaching and Cooperative Learning

• Put students in groups of five or six. Assign each group a common theme or character trait (such as honesty, dedication, integrity). Have each group read selected works across genres and historical periods that deal with the assigned theme. Have each group make a presentation to the class outlining the similarities and differences in the treatment of the theme.

Storytelling

• With expression and passion, read aloud selections from a variety of literary works so that students can appreciate the beauty and aesthetic appeal of the literature.

• Have students independently read selected literary works (such as poetry, short stories, novels) for the purpose of enjoying the aesthetics of the literature.

• Use bibliotherapy to help students understand and deal with their life experiences. For example, if a student's parents are going through a divorce or if a student has lost a family member or close friend, have that student read a story or book about a person who may be experiencing the same thing. This activity requires the teacher to have some knowledge of books that would be appropriate for the age and grade level. Consult the school's media specialist for recommendations.

Writing and Journals

- Have students read literature in which the major character faces an ethical dilemma such as choosing between right and wrong. Students determine how the character resolved the dilemma and then write a journal entry regarding whether they would have resolved the situation in similar fashion and, if not, what they would have done differently.

REFLECTION AND APPLICATION

Which strategies can I use to engage students' brains so that they choose to read widely?

Standard/Objective: _____

_____

_____.

Activity: _____

_____

_____.

Standard/Objective: _____

_____

_____.

Activity: _____

_____

_____.

Standard/Objective: _____

_____

_____.

Activity: _____

_____

_____.

Standard/Objective: _____

_____

_____.

Activity: _____

_____

_____.

Standard/Objective: _____

_____

_____.

Activity: _____

_____

_____.

8

Reading Strategically

Information becomes memorable when it is presented in both the linguistic and nonlinguistic modes of the visual organizer.

—Marzano, Gaddy, & Dean, 2000

Mrs. Dawson is beginning a unit on the Revolutionary War. She engages students in completing a KNL chart on which students brainstorm what they already Know and what they Need to know about this war. This gives students a purpose for learning about the topic. Following this unit, students will complete the KNL chart by brainstorming all of the concepts they have Learned.

As students read the chapters in the unit, Mrs. Dawson will equip them with a variety of strategies that good readers use to comprehend texts. They will begin with an SQ3R procedure during which they will work with a partner or in a small group to Survey each chapter in an effort to ascertain specifically what they will be learning. They will peruse captions, bold headings, charts, diagrams, and italicized or bolded key vocabulary concepts. They will then formulate additional questions that they would like answered by turning the bold headings into Questions. Students will then Read the text for the purpose of answering the questions, Recite the answers to the questions in their own words, and then periodically Review the information to facilitate memory.

This is just a small sampling of the activities in which students should engage in their attempt to understand texts. Refer to the plethora of activities contained in the following chapters to assist students in improving their word identification and comprehension skills when reading both fiction and nonfiction texts: Chapter 2: "Phonics Instruction," Chapter 4: "Vocabulary Instruction," and Chapter 5: "Text Comprehension Instruction."

RELEVANT RESEARCH

Students apply a wide range of strategies to comprehend, interpret, evaluate, and appreciate texts. They draw on their prior experience, their interactions with other readers and writers, their knowledge of word meaning and of other texts, their word identification strategies, and their understanding of textual features (e.g., sound-letter correspondence, sentence structure, context, graphics (NCTE/IRA, 1996, Standard III).

Without a systematic approach for managing the information overload (facts, names, figures, charts, old and new concepts) in textbooks, students lose their motivation and ability to navigate through the text (Strong et al., 2002).

There appear to be six basic formats of nonfiction text structure: (1) a comparison structure, which looks at the similarities and differences in two or more ideas or concepts; (2) a sequence or timeline structure, which presents events in a comprehensible or chronological order; (3) a topic description structure, which places facts or events in a simple order; (4) a cycle structure, which shows patterns or trends that often end up in the same place they began; (5) a problem-solution structure, which deals with the effects of a solution on a given problem; and (6) a cause-effect structure, which shows the casual relationships between an event or idea and the events and ideas that follow it (Strong et al., 2002).

Asking students' questions serves three purposes: (1) to focus the learning, (2) to gain the interest of students, and (3) to guide the learning process (Strong et al., 2002).

The *cloze procedure* can be an effective technique for all students (including those with learning disabilities) because it provides a structured activity during which students can use context clues to fill in missing words (Bender, 2002).

Information becomes memorable when it is presented in both the linguistic and nonlinguistic modes of the visual organizer (Marzano, Gaddy, & Dean, 2000).

Visual organizers or semantic graphs facilitate memory and achievement for science or social studies passages (National Reading Panel, 2000).

When students use the complex process of synthesizing information, they notice how the details can be pieced together to form a whole (Harvey & Goudvis, 2000).

Essential questions focus on the major concepts of the content, originate during the process of learning, and generate additional questions (Wiggins & McTighe, 1998).

Students can break information into meaningful segments, see connections among those segments, and make those segments easier to remember when graphic organizers are used (Parry & Gregory, 1998).

STRATEGIC ACTIVITIES

Objective: Read strategically to comprehend, interpret, evaluate, and appreciate texts

Brainstorming and Discussion

- Have students make predictions before reading a literary selection regarding what it is about. Then have students read to confirm or disprove their predictions. Following the reading, have students create questions to test the comprehension of their classmates. These higher-level questions should be ones that require students to comprehend, analyze, interpret, or show their appreciation for the text.

Drawing and Artwork

- Have students make an artistic interpretation of the main idea or major scenes of a poem or story they have read. Students might choose to produce collages, watercolor paintings, or colorful drawings to represent their interpretations.

Graphic Organizers, Semantic Maps, and Word Webs

- Before reading a selection or content-area text, have students complete the KNL chart found in Chapter 5. This chart will help students set purposes for reading by brainstorming what they already <u>K</u>now about a given topic, what they <u>N</u>eed to know, and, following the completion of the unit, what they <u>L</u>earned.

- Refer to the graphic organizers in Chapter 5: "Text Comprehension Instruction" for additional examples of ways to help students understand text structure.

- Have students use the following visual organizers to assist them in understanding the six basic formats of text structure (Strong et al., 2002)

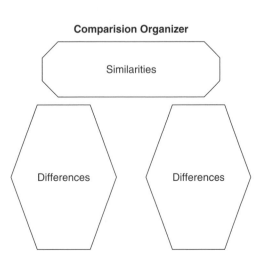

Comparision Organizer

Similarities

Differences   Differences

Sequence Organizer

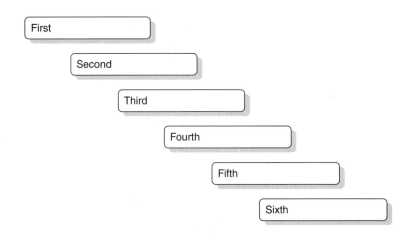

First

Second

Third

Fourth

Fifth

Sixth

Topic Description Organizer

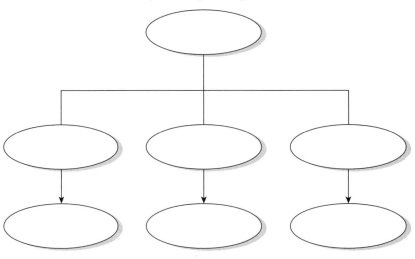

Cycle Organizer

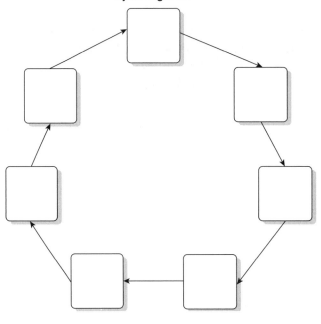

Problem-Solution Organizer

Problem	Solution	Effect

Cause-Effect Organizer

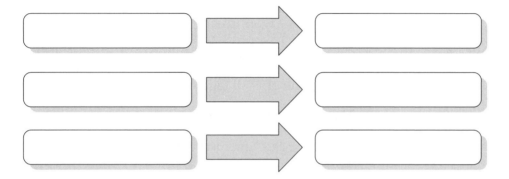

Metaphors, Analogies, and Similes

- Explain to students the concept that a main idea and details can be compared to a table's top and its legs. The top of the table represents the main idea of a story, and the legs are the details. Just like a table's legs support its top, a story's details support its main idea. Have students draw a table and its legs. Following the reading of a literary work, have them write one significant detail on each leg of the table and the main idea on the top (Tate, 2003).

Music, Rhythm, Rhyme, and Rap

- Teach parts of speech and sentence structure through music. Create a song, rhythm, rhyme, or rap to teach a particular grammatical concept.

For example, Gwendolyn Bolt, Reading Specialist, created the following raps to teach the function of verbs:

Verb Rap

Verbs show action.

Indeed they do.

But we have to know a rule or two.

Present tense means here and now.

So add "s" if it is a singular noun.

When it's plural, don't get caught.

Be sure to leave the old "s" off.

A snail moves slow.

The horse gallops fast.

Rabbits jump.

The dog chases a cat.

The monkey swings.

Three worms wiggle.

A bear climbs a tree.

The girls all giggle.

The action is past and gone on by.

Add "d" or "ed" and don't ask why.

Jeffery mixed the paint.

Susan painted boards.

Mark washed the brush.

Carlos finished the chores.

Change "help" to "helped."

"Walk" to "walked."

"Pull" to "pulled," and "talk" to "talked."

The rap goes on until we're through.

Now it's your turn to try one or two.

SOURCE: Used with permission of Gwendolyn G. Bolt, Reading Specialist, Greenview Elementary, Greenville, SC.

• Purchase prerecorded CDs of songs that teach or reinforce reading and language arts skills. For example, on his CD *Shake, Rattle and Read,* Jack Hartmann leads children in singing songs that teach skills from ABCs to vowel sounds. Order Jack Hartmann's CDs at his Web site: www .JackHartmann.com.

• Another person who has numerous songs, rhymes, and chants for teaching reading and language arts skills is Dr. Jean Feldman. Order her CDs at www.drjean.org.

Project-Based and Problem-Based Instruction

- Have students use the before reading, during reading, and after reading Survey, Question, Read, Recite, Review (SQ3R) procedure outlined in the introduction to this chapter to assist students in comprehending content-area texts.

Reciprocal Teaching and Cooperative Learning

- Have students form book clubs with other students by selecting a book (from a predetermined list) that all students in the club choose to read. Provide time for students to have discussions with other members of the club regarding designated chapters in the book they have selected.

Storytelling

- Use an oral cloze technique by reading aloud text from a narrative or content-area text while students follow the text, reading silently. Periodically pause and allow students to say the next word in the text. This technique enables students to track print and hear whole phrases of text read in a fluent way.

Writing and Journals

- Select a reading passage and delete every seventh word (not including such words as *a, the,* and *an*). Replace each deleted word with a blank line. Have students read the passage silently and supply a word that would make sense in each blank. Have them read the selection aloud to a partner, who checks to be sure the inserted words make sense in the passage.

Adaptation: Rather than deleting every seventh word, omit content-area terms or key vocabulary words.

REFLECTION AND APPLICATION

> ## Which strategies can I use to engage students' brains so that they read strategically?

Standard/Objective: _____

_____

_____.

Activity: _____

_____

_____.

Standard/Objective: _____

_____

_____.

Activity: _____

_____

_____.

Standard/Objective: _____

_____

_____.

Activity: _____

_____

_____.

Standard/Objective: _____

_____

_____.

Activity: _____

_____

_____.

Standard/Objective: _____

_____

_____.

Activity: _____

_____

_____.

9

Adjusting Language

Good readers read with a purpose in mind.

—Partnership for Reading, 2000

Try this project with your class: Have students work in cooperative groups to create a TV commercial designed to persuade their classmates to accept a particular point of view, such as "All students should wear uniforms." Each group must decide on the point of view they will take, brainstorm logical arguments in favor of that point of view, and then come up with a clever way to advertise their arguments. They will then present their commercial to the class, integrating the appropriate use of visuals or role play. Students are graded on a rubric that the class has developed. This rubric might include the following dimensions: (1) the presentation format was effective for communicating information, (2) a minimum of three reasons were given to support the point of view, and (3) logical arguments to support each of the three reasons were included. By developing and presenting their commercial, students will use written, visual, and spoken language to communicate with audiences for the purpose of persuasion.

The 20 brain-compatible strategies referenced in this book can be used to engage students' brains because they incorporate all four of the major learning modalities: visual (visuals, visualization), auditory (brainstorming and discussion, reciprocal teaching), tactile (drawing, manipulatives, writing), and kinesthetic (movement, role play, work study). Students can use these strategies to persuade, entertain, inform, and describe through a variety of real-life purposes.

RELEVANT RESEARCH

Students adjust their use of spoken, written, and visual language (e.g., conventions, style, vocabulary) to communicate effectively with a variety of audiences and for different purposes (NCTE/IRA, 1996, Standard IV).

Because note taking is essential for success in the world of academics, it should be taught directly in a variety of modes and be modeled, practiced, coached, and applied (Strong et al., 2002).

Good readers read with a purpose in mind, whether that purpose is gathering information, meeting course requirements, or entertaining themselves (Partnership for Reading, 2001).

The ability to communicate effectively in writing is an essential life skill that corresponds to the writer's needs, purposes, and interests (Routman, 2000).

Having students read and study in the genre in which they are assigned to write will make them better writers (Routman, 2000).

When students read nonfiction, they must decode and interpret visual elements such as charts, timelines, graphs, maps, and diagrams (Routman, 2000).

Visually beautiful nonfiction texts can be appealing to students because they include imagery that is supported by text and that is descriptive in nature (Routman, 2000).

When teachers value the language, cultural experiences, and background of students, school becomes part of life and a place where learning is relevant (Routman, 2000).

Teachers should select nonfiction books for classroom use that have clear descriptions and visual aids that enhance the meaning of the text (Zarnowski, 1995).

Mapping helps students understand verbal, nonverbal, concrete, or abstract concepts because maps integrate both the visual and the verbal (Sousa, 1995).

If students are to communicate well in life, they must become visually literate (Moline, 1995).

Affirmation, contribution, purpose, power, and satisfaction are the five motivators for inviting students to learn (Tomlinson, 1992).

When students have opportunities to read various types of writing and when teachers use conferences and mini-lessons to introduce students to new genres, students recognize real-life purposes for their writing (Atwell, 1987).

STRATEGIC ACTIVITIES

Objective: Adjust language for effective communication

Brainstorming and Discussion

• Select a controversial topic related to a unit of study, such as *Should the draft be reinstated?* Have students work in pairs. Each student in the pair takes an opposing side of the controversial issue and develops logical arguments in support of their point of view. Once the arguments have been written, have each pair participate in a debate before the entire class. Have students decide which student has the most convincing argument in support of his or her position.

Drawing and Artwork

- Have students create a visual depicting information gleaned from a chapter or unit of study. Students could have options regarding which form their visual will take, such as a drawing, collage, watercolor, graphic organizer, and so forth.

Humor

- Have students create cartoons, comic strips, jokes, riddles, or puns based on course content. Because the brain needs occasional downtime during an intense period of learning, have students volunteer to tell their original jokes or bring in related jokes to share with the class for the purpose of entertainment.

Music, Rhythm, Rhyme, and Rap

- Have students work individually or in small groups to create a song, rhyme, or rap which demonstrates their understanding of a concept taught. Have them perform their original compositions for the entire class.

Project-Based and Problem-Based Instruction

- Engage students in a project in which they must present factual information from a content-area chapter or unit of study in the following three ways: in written form, which could include a well-developed paper or the development of an appropriate graphic organizer; in visual form, which could include a poster, drawing, or PowerPoint presentation; and in spoken form in which students give an oral presentation to the class. Students should not simply stand and read their papers aloud to the class. They should use their creativity to prepare and deliver a presentation that holds the attention of their classmates.

- Have students prepare a reader's theatre from a story previously read. Reader's theatre is a dramatization in which members of the class read the dialogue of various characters in a story, while a narrator sets the scene and provides the background information for the audience.

Storytelling

- Have students enhance their public-speaking skills by preparing a retelling of a story that they have read independently. Students retell the first few parts of the story to a peer, cooperative group, or the entire class and should do this in such a convincing and entertaining way that classmates will want to read the entire book for themselves.

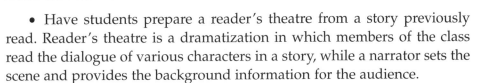

Technology

- Have students develop a PowerPoint presentation that depicts visually what they have learned from a chapter or unit of study. Have them present this to the class. Grade presentations for visual appeal as well as for accuracy of information.

Visualization and Guided Imagery

- Have students write a descriptive paragraph and read it aloud to the class. The paragraph should be so well written that fellow students can actually visualize the events taking place in the paragraph because good readers consistently visualize scenes in stories read.

Writing and Journals

- Engage students in *quick writes*—short opportunities for students to write brief answers to designated questions related to course content, such as "Write two synonyms for the word *dilapidated.*"

- Consistently provide students with cross-curricular opportunities to write for a variety of purposes. Students' writing should inform, persuade, describe, or entertain depending on the task assigned.

- Have students write a letter as if they were a historical figure or a storybook character. Each student's writing should reflect knowledge of the character traits of the figure or character portrayed. For example, students could write as if they are Brian from the story *Hatchet,* whose plane crashes in the Canadian wilderness. They could write about how they would handle the situation if they were in Brian's situation.

REFLECTION AND APPLICATION

> **Which strategies can I use to engage students' brains so that they adjust their use of language for effective communication?**

Standard/Objective: _____

_____

_____.

Activity: _____

_____

_____.

Standard/Objective: _____

_____

_____.

Activity: _____

_____

_____.

Standard/Objective: _____

_____

_____.

Activity: _____

_____

_____.

Standard/Objective: _____

_____

_____.

Activity: _____

_____

_____.

Standard/Objective: _____

_____

_____.

Activity: _____

_____

_____.

10

Writing Strategically

Writing does not begin with deskwork but with lifework.

—Calkins, 1994, p. 3

I once heard a speaker say that he had met people who were fluent readers but were not good writers, but he had never met a good writer who was not also a good reader. Because reading and writing are complementary processes, it stands to reason that the writing activities contained in this chapter will facilitate the reading abilities of students as well.

Whether people are making a grocery list, answering an e-mail, or practicing the lost art of letter writing, communicating in written form is an essential life skill. The SCANS Report (1991) even lists writing as one of the basic skills required for success in the real world of work. Brain research also relates that when a person is writing, particularly in small chunks of information, memory is facilitated. Have you ever written a list of groceries that you would like to buy at the store and then forgot and left the list at home? Isn't it interesting that you could still remember many of the things on the list when you got to the store?

All teachers, regardless of content area, are writing teachers. A student can write the steps to the solution of a math problem, the three causes of the Civil War, or the results observed during a science experiment. Chapman and King (2003) delineated four writing goals for each student: (1) to apply the information learned, (2) to write and think critically, (3) to write and think creatively, and (4) to solve actual, real-world problems.

RELEVANT RESEARCH

Students employ a wide range of strategies as they write and use different writing process elements appropriately to communicate with different audiences and for different purposes (NCTE/IRA, 1996, Standard V).

Whereas preschool students use "novice writing" and first-graders use invented spelling, older students write independently as they increase vocabulary and their knowledge of syntax and orthography (Wolfe & Nevills, 2004).

When students write, their brains reverse the reading process. Rather than responding first to external visual stimuli, the brain starts with internal thoughts, selects appropriate vocabulary for those thoughts, and then produces the symbols for the words in writing (Wolfe & Nevills, 2004).

Teaching students to form mental images while reading can have a positive effect on their writing (Miller, 2002).

When students have the opportunity to write, they are allowed to think one more time about what they have read, this time on paper (Harvey & Goudvis, 2000).

Students are able to make sense of complicated pieces of information when they write down what is being presented, what they are observing, or what they are thinking (Jensen, 2000).

If students are to become better writers, they must study and read in the genre in which they are assigned to write (Routman, 2000).

When students write short, succinct phrases during note taking, short- and long-term memory is increased because writing encourages the brain to remember information to be recalled later (Hadwin et al., 1999).

Newspaper articles, editorials, short stories, and posters are vehicles through which students can express their emotional memories in writing (Sprenger, 1999).

Shared writing, interactive writing, guided writing or writing workshops, and independent writing are the four types of writing inherent in the Ohio State University Literacy Collaborative Framework (Fountas & Pinnell, 1996).

Hardware and software tools enable students to write creatively and scientifically (Uchida, Cetron, & McKenzie, 1996).

Students must write for a variety of real-life purposes and become involved in the total act of reading and writing (Au, 1994).

STRATEGIC ACTIVITIES

Objective: Write strategically for a variety of audiences and purposes

Brainstorming and Discussion

- Have students use descriptive writing whenever they want to create distinct, visual images of a person, place, thing, or event. To be an effective descriptive writer, students must learn to use verbs, adverbs, and adjectives that paint pictures in the brain. Before writing a descriptive paragraph on an assigned topic, have students work in small groups to brainstorm possible descriptive parts of speech to be used in the paragraph. For example, have students brainstorm and then write a descriptive character analysis of a storybook or historical figure.

- Have students write persuasively in an attempt to change the beliefs, feelings, attitudes, and behaviors of the reader. Students should clearly state their opinion and then give facts that prove or support their opinion. In this regard, students can write across the curriculum as they produce posters, editorials, commercials, letters, and book reviews related to the content being studied.

Drawing and Artwork

- Have students draw a scene, such as one that depicts the main idea of a story they have read, before writing about it. This illustration will assist the brain in forming the vivid visual images that are so necessary for effective descriptive writing. Have students then write several paragraphs that vividly describe the scene they have drawn.

Humor

- Have fun with students by having them use expository writing procedures to describe an everyday process such as brushing one's teeth, putting on a sweater, or making a peanut butter and jelly sandwich. Have students pretend that they are explaining the process to an alien who has never actually seen or experienced it. The student must include every detail in the most explanatory way. Once students have finished writing, have them read the procedure aloud as another student attempts to follow the directions. Point out how many steps we all take for granted and actually omit when writing a procedure for someone else to follow!

Metaphors, Analogies, and Similes

- Read a story or poem that incorporates the use of imagery, metaphors, analogies, and similes. An example would be *The Fog* by

Robert Frost, which begins *The fog comes in on little cat feet.* Then have students incorporate these same elements to enhance their descriptive writing.

Music, Rhythm, Rhyme, and Rap

- Have students draw visualizations or mental images while listening to a nature CD. Following the drawing, have students write about their images. Encourage them to brainstorm vocabulary that can be used to describe their visualizations vividly and to incorporate their vocabulary into their writing; an example of such writing is *The stream meanders down the rugged terrain.*

Storytelling

- Storytelling is one of the best ways to help students experience narrative writing. When students write a narrative, they are telling a story. That story may be in the form of a journal, diary, short story, essay, or book. Consistently involve students in cross-curricular opportunities to write in narrative form.

Visualization and Guided Imagery

- Visualization is a strategy used during descriptive writing. Have students form mental images before they begin to write descriptively.

Visuals

- Create a spelling word wall by posting words that students use constantly but misspell in their writing, such as *because, where,* or *want.* This wall can serve as an easy reference for encouraging the accurate spelling of common words.

Writing and Journals

- Examine students' writing for areas that need improvement. Conduct a writing workshop to provide students with direct instruction in a particular writing element that needs improvement, such as using descriptive adjectives.

- Have students engage in expository writing as they explain a step-by-step procedure, retell a story, or explain how to accomplish a task. Students should know how to inform or explain; to remember an event, procedure, or process in sequential order; to provide accurate and specific explanations; and to write for an audience of readers who must follow the written procedure or retell the information (Chapman & King, 2003).

• Provide time daily for students to write in a diary or journal about incidents that are important to them. Personal journals are not typically graded but allow students the opportunity to hone their writing skills as they describe incidents that happened at home, reflect on class assignments, or express feelings and emotions related to an event.

• Have students brainstorm synonyms for words that are overused in their writing. Post the alternative words on chart paper and encourage them to incorporate these into their writing. Refer to the article "Said Webs: Remedy for Tired Words" by Kathryn L. Laframboise (2000) to find 18 alternatives to the word *said,* such as bragged, murmured, muttered, responded, and so on.

• The four types of writing inherent in the Ohio State Literacy Collaborative Framework (Fountas & Pinnell, 1996) are as follows: shared writing, interactive writing, guided writing or writing workshop, and independent writing. Refer to the above reference for specific procedures.

REFLECTION AND APPLICATION

**Which strategies can I use to engage
students' brains so that they write strategically?**

Standard/Objective: _____

_____

_____.

Activity: _____

_____

_____.

Standard/Objective: _____

_____

_____.

Activity: _____

_____

_____.

Standard/Objective: _____

_____

_____.

Activity: _____

_____

_____.

Standard/Objective: _____

_____

_____.

Activity: _____

_____

_____.

Standard/Objective: _____

_____

_____.

Activity: _____

_____

_____.

11

Applying Knowledge of Language Structure

Students must see the relevancy of language structure for learning to occur; therefore, teaching these skills in isolation will not work.

—Anderson, 2004

When I was a classroom teacher years ago, I taught reading as a separate subject. Then we would put the reading books away, and I would teach English. What brain research tells us is that the brain learns best when the learning is connected in real-life contexts. Therefore, interdisciplinary instruction is brain-compatible. Students are best taught English skills not from a separate worksheet but within the context of narrative and expository texts, the medium through which those skills are expected to be applied.

I was recently asked to teach a model lesson to a class of fifth-grade students. The objective was to introduce the concept of keeping a personal journal while simultaneously reviewing common and proper nouns. To hook the students emotionally into the lesson, I introduced them to one of the most important personal journals of all time, *The Diary of Anne Frank.* I explained how her diary reflected the personal feelings and emotions of a young girl hiding above a warehouse for two and a half years, scarcely able to talk or move for fear of being discovered by the German gestapo and taken to a concentration camp during World War II. As I read emotional excerpts from the diary, students reflected on how they would feel in that same situation. We also discussed which words in the diary would be capitalized, such as gestapo and German and why.

Integrating that English skill into the context of emotional, authentic writing helped to ensure that this lesson, and the skill taught, would be long remembered.

RELEVANT RESEARCH

Students apply knowledge of language structure, language conventions, (e.g., spelling and punctuation), media techniques, figurative language, and genre to create, critique, and discuss print and non-print texts (NCTE/IRA, 1996, Standard VI).

Spelling words should be selected from students' writing and should be those words frequently used in students' writing vocabularies. Content-area words do not make good spelling words because they are typically not high-frequency words (Anderson, 2004).

Appropriate grammar and sentence structure should be modeled for preschool children instead of being directly taught (Wolfe & Nevills, 2004).

Students must see the relevancy of language structure for learning to occur; therefore, teaching these skills in isolation will not work (Anderson, 2004).

Capitalization and punctuation are effectively taught within the context of modeled writing, mini-lessons, and the actual act of reading (Anderson, 2004).

Language skills for the preschool child are best developed as a child works and plays and not through isolated skill development, worksheets, or formal phonics instruction (Wolfe & Nevills, 2004).

When phonetic or invented spelling is allowed during the first draft of a creative writing piece or during free writing, the student has an increased opportunity to express thoughts without fear of making a mistake (Chapman & King, 2003).

Students' speaking vocabulary supercedes their writing vocabulary (Chapman & King, 2003).

Poetry can be one of the most popular sources of metaphors and similes (Blachowicz & Fisher, 2002).

The use of figurative language is both natural and necessary because an adult uses more than 500,000 figures of speech annually (Petrosky, 1980).

STRATEGIC ACTIVITIES

Objective: Apply knowledge of language structure and conventions to create, critique, and discuss print and nonprint texts

Brainstorming and Discussion

• Introduce students to a variety of genres such as mystery, historical, and realistic fiction; folktales; biographies; and informational text. As you read aloud stories from the various genres or have students read them independently, identify elements that are characteristic of a particular type of literature. Then have students imitate the genre by using these same characteristics in their personal writing.

• Hold individual student-teacher conferences for the purpose of discussing each student's writing. Focus on areas of individual need and set goals for the language structures you would like to see incorporated consistently into each student's writing.

Metaphors, Analogies, and Similes

• Have students read poems that contain examples of metaphors, analogies, and similes such as those in Shel Silverstein's *Where the Sidewalk Ends.* Facilitate a whole class discussion on the meaning of each poem.

Movement

• After a discussion of four types of punctuation, have students "walk the punctuation." Have students walk around the room while reading aloud a poem or story. Write the poem or story on the board so that it serves as a visual. Have students stop in their tracks at the sign of a period, pause in their walk when they encounter a comma, shrug their shoulders when they see a question mark, and jump once for an exclamation point. Watch how easily students learn the function of these punctuation marks.

• Students can comprehend numerous language structures and conventions by using the following activity. Create a sentence containing the language structures and conventions you wish to teach, such as *"Brain-compatible strategies create classrooms where every student can learn."* Write each separate word in the sentence on a different piece of construction paper large enough for all students to see. Have one student come to the front of the room for every word in the sentence. For example, in the previous italicized sentence, 10 students should come to the front of the room. Randomly assign each student one word to hold up and show to the class. Then the fun begins! Some possible applications include:

1. Have students arrange themselves in an order that forms a logical sentence. Note that there are several possibilities for forming sentences.

2. Have students in the class arrange the students in the front of the room so that they form a sentence.

3. Have the simple subject take one step forward. Have the complex subject step forward.

4. Have the simple predicate take one step forward. Have the complex predicate step forward.

5. Have specific parts of speech step forward, such as all nouns, verbs, prepositions, and so on.

6. Have a prepositional phrase step forward.

By the time students in the class have seen the specific language conventions displayed, sentence structure is retained and remembered.

Project-Based and Problem-Based Instruction

• As content is taught across the curriculum, have students show what they have learned through the creation of authentic projects. These projects should incorporate the use of grammar and language structure and may include posters, brochures, newspapers, videos, audiotapes, PowerPoint presentations, graphic organizers, and so on.

Reciprocal Teaching and Cooperative Learning

• Give a mini-lesson that teaches a particular language structure such as compound sentences or the use of descriptive adjectives. Hold students responsible for incorporating into their writing any language structure that has been taught. Have students edit one another's writing samples in search of that specific language structure.

• Select and read aloud several short sentences from students' writing. Keep the students' names anonymous. Have students work with a partner to expand each sentence by adding adverbs, adjectives, and clauses that make the writing more interesting and expressive. Have students read their new and improved sentences to the class.

Storytelling

• Specific children's books can be used to teach and reinforce grammar and language structure. These stories can be used as read-alouds and for subsequent instruction to launch students into an authentic study of language. Some suggested titles are as follows:

A Cache of Jewels (collective nouns)   Ruth Heller

Many Luscious Lollipops (adjectives)   Ruth Heller

The King Who Rained (figurative language)   Fred Gwynne

Visuals

• Display high-frequency words or words consistently used in students' writing on the wall so that students can have visuals to assist them with spelling as they write.

Writing and Journals

• As you observe students' writing, identify areas of strength in their language structure and areas in need of improvement. Present mini-lessons that model the language structures needed. Encourage students to incorporate these structures into their own writing that they share and discuss with a close partner.

• As students write, hold them accountable for any spelling words and language structures in their writing that have been taught. Students should be expected to spell these words or use these structures correctly at all times.

REFLECTION AND APPLICATION

> **Which strategies can I use to engage students' brains so that they can apply knowledge of language structure to texts?**

Standard/Objective: _____

_____

_____.

Activity: _____

_____

_____.

Standard/Objective: _____

_____

_____.

Activity: _____

_____

_____.

Standard/Objective: _____

_____

_____.

Activity: _____

_____

_____.

Standard/Objective: _____

_____

_____.

Activity: _____

_____

_____.

Standard/Objective: _____

_____

_____.

Activity: _____

_____

_____.

Conducting Research

When students solve problems, they test hypotheses that can result in divergent thinking.

—Marzano, Pickering, & Pollack, 2001

When students are posing and solving real-world problems, they are using the brain in the way it was intended to be used. The primary purpose of the brain is to help its owner survive. Therefore, information gleaned when the brain is involved in those activities that are necessary for survival, such as completing projects or solving problems, is understood and remembered. Westwater and Wolfe (2000) relate that information the brain considers crucial is much more likely to be remembered and retrieved than that information the brain decides is of little significance.

It probably wouldn't take you very long to recall a project you completed or a problem you solved when you were in school. In eighth grade, I recall going to the creek across the street from my house, putting some creek water into a baby food jar, bringing the jar to school, and placing a drop of the water under the microscope. To this day, I can vividly recall the paramecium swimming around in the drop of water. The following strategies can be used to assist students in conducting research on subjects of interest to them and gathering the necessary data to answer the questions posed in the research.

RELEVANT RESEARCH

Students conduct research on issues and interests by generating ideas and questions and by posing problems. They gather, evaluate, and synthesize data from a variety of sources (e.g., print and nonprint texts, artifacts, people) to communicate their discoveries in ways that suit their purpose and audience (NCTE/IRA, 1996, Standard VII).

Projects enable students who have mastered a skill or who are experts on a topic to develop a special plan so that they can grow in knowledge (Chapman & King, 2003).

Good readers use context clues while reading to enable them to acquire expanded vocabularies (Gallagher, 2003).

Student Choice Contract Models enable students to present a proposal to their teacher for completion of a project. The students provide their original project idea, rationales, procedures, and final products (Chapman & King, 2003, p. 63).

Good readers figure out whether the answers to their questions are explicitly stated in the text or whether the answer must be inferred from the text, their own background, or an outside source (Miller, 2002).

When students are solving problems, they test hypotheses that can result in divergent thinking and an exploration of various possibilities (Marzano, Pickering, & Pollack, 2001).

Projects provide opportunities for students to build knowledge and skill and demonstrate their understanding of narrative and expository text in a number of ways and for authentic purposes (Luongo-Orlando, 2001).

When students conduct projects or solve problems, they are being prepared for the real world of work because projects and short-term contracts are replacing full-time jobs (Sternberg & Grigorenko, 2000).

When information that students are learning is linked to authentic, real-life experiences, students remember and can apply the information in meaningful contexts (Westwater & Wolfe, 2000).

Effective teachers build on what students already know as they integrate both approaches and strategies to encourage students to problem solve, self-monitor, and become independent thinkers (Routman, 2000).

Students need opportunities to investigate complicated real-life problems, to learn from mistakes, to work with peers, to reflect on what they are experiencing, and to be made responsible for their own learning (Revenaugh, 2000).

When teachers teach for understanding, students are able to use their knowledge and skill in context. Research, then, is important, but only if it leads students to information that is worth knowing (Wiggins & McTighe, 1998).

STRATEGIC ACTIVITIES

Objective: Conduct research by gathering, evaluating, and synthesizing data

Brainstorming and Discussion

- Have students brainstorm all of the nonfiction sources that can be used when a person is solving a real-life problem, conducting research, or completing a project. Those sources can be categorized as the following: primary sources, print materials, information technology, and other. Primary sources could include interviews, surveys, speeches, journals and newspapers. Print materials could include reference books, nonfiction texts, encyclopedias, and newspaper and magazine articles. Information technology could include CD-ROMS, Internet sites, videos, movies and TV shows. Other sources include guest speakers, field trips, maps, and graphics (Luongo-Orlando, 2001).

Drawing and Artwork

- Have students solve word problems in mathematics by drawing pictures to represent the various steps. Each drawing must truly illustrate the step it represents. Have students then use symbols to solve the problem.

- During the study of a particular country or continent, have students design a travel brochure delineating the most important places to visit and resources that location has to offer. Each brochure should include visuals as well as print material.

Manipulatives

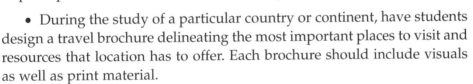

- Involve students in experiments and lab work that will enable them to solve a problem or make a discovery. Have them form hypotheses and make predictions as to the outcome of the experiment before conducting it. Have them conduct the experiment, analyze the data, and then form conclusions as to the outcome. Have students write up each phase of the process so that they can integrate their descriptive writing skills into their science content.

- As a practical homework assignment, have students make a favorite dish by following a recipe. Have each student bring in the recipe so that you can be sure it includes fractions. Have students calculate the ingredients in the recipe as if it were doubled and then calculate it again as if it were halved. Have them make the recipe in a half portion for homework and bring it to class to share.

Project-Based and Problem-Based Instruction

- Provide students with opportunities to study a subject in depth through project-based learning. Projects should enable them to process and use the information gleaned and extend the learning opportunity to a specific area of study. For example, students are given the assignment to produce a product that will show their understanding of the Civil War. Some students may elect to make a PowerPoint presentation, and others will publish a Civil War newspaper.

- Give students an opportunity to solve a problem related to the school or its surrounding community. For example, students could work in small groups to brainstorm ways to increase parental participation in school activities and to design a plan for implementation.

- Have students participate in a service learning project in which they meet curricular goals and objectives while simultaneously performing a service in their school or community. This project enables students to gather data regarding the service they are to perform and analyze and utilize those data in accomplishing the project. For example, at one school I visited in Tennessee, Scott County High School students designed and constructed, and currently operate, an entire natural history museum on the school grounds. Students actually researched the historical events that would be included, constructed the museum, designed the layout of the exhibits including the artwork, and now serve as guides for the exhibits when the museum is open to the public. Imagine how many cross-curricular objectives were met by the time students had completed this inspiring project. Imagine what an inspiration the students are for the larger community.

- Have students interview a family or community member regarding a topic of interest.

- Have students survey classmates to ascertain their opinion about a topic with questions such as *Who would you vote for in the presidential election?* Students may then create graphs to indicate the results of the survey.

- Have students solve math problems by posing them in real-world contexts. For example, to teach students the use of patterns, relations, and functions in mathematics, give them the following problem.

You went to Blockbuster video store to rent a movie. The cost of the rental was $3.95, and you could keep the video for one week. The charge for not returning the video on time is $2.98 per day for every day beyond the due date. You kept the video for 11 days. How much will you owe to Blockbuster? Design a chart that shows how much you will owe each day for at least 8 days past the due date.

 ## Technology

- Have students research issues of interest by accessing Web sites and gathering, evaluating, and synthesizing the data derived from these sites.

Writing and Journals

• Give students several pages from the newspaper and ask them to find five words that are unfamiliar to them. Have them write the sentence in which they found each unfamiliar word and predict its definition. Have students consult with other students or dictionaries to see whether their predictions are accurate.

REFLECTION AND APPLICATION

> ## Which strategies can I use to engage students' brains when conducting research?

Standard/Objective: _____
_____
_____.

Activity: _____
_____
_____.

Standard/Objective: _____
_____
_____.

Activity: _____
_____
_____.

Standard/Objective: _____
_____
_____.

Activity: _____
_____
_____.

Standard/Objective: _____
_____
_____.

Activity: _____
_____
_____.

Standard/Objective: _____
_____
_____.

Activity: _____
_____
_____.

13

Using Technological and Informational Resources

Students must not only know how to access the wide variety of information technology affords us but must also be able to process that information.

—Uchida et al., 1996

From the year 4 B.C. to the year A.D. 1900, recorded information in the world is said to have doubled. From the year 1900 to the year 1964, it doubled again. Amazingly, what had taken more than 1,900 years the first time around took only 64 years the second time. Depending on which source you believe, information today is doubling every few months to every two years. Some authorities even suggest that every 50 to 60 days, information on the World Wide Web doubles.

Is it any wonder, then, that if a teacher's major task is to fill the brains of students with myriad facts to be memorized, the battle is lost before it is waged? Teachers' instructional methodologies must center around assisting students to determine what information is essential in completing an instructional task and teaching students how to locate that information. In this decade, students can avail themselves of technological and informational resources that were not even considered in the past. E-mail, video streaming, computer databases, and video conferencing are only a few of the viable options that students have for gathering, organizing, and synthesizing information in an effort to transmit knowledge.

RELEVANT RESEARCH

Students use a variety of technological and informational resources (e.g., libraries, databases, computer networks, video) to gather and synthesize information and to create and communicate knowledge (NCTE/IRA, 1996, Standard VIII).

Environmental print, such as road signs, fast-food logos, and billboards, in the real-life contexts of the classroom and surrounding areas are great sources for incidental word learning (Rasinski & Padak, 2001).

Collaborative telelearning enables students to become actively engaged in cross-continental learning sessions with other students around the globe (Andrews & Marshall, 2000).

To reduce the effects of the digital divide, ensure that all students have access to computers by doing some of the following: (1) having computers available in public libraries and community centers; (2) allowing students to have access to school computers by extending the hours that the school is open; (3) allowing parents to check out laptop computers; and (4) providing funding for training, support, and culturally sensitive software (Holloway, 2000).

High-tech products do not compare to good teaching, small class sizes, and a curriculum that challenges the brains of students (Healy, 1998).

When people assume that adding a computer to a classroom will automatically increase learning, we are shown how little society truly understands the dynamic interactions between teachers and students (Healy, 1998).

Because the early years should be used for developing students' language, social skills, and attention span, computers should probably not be introduced into classrooms until age seven (Healy, 1998).

Technology can be used to enrich the curriculum because it provides new knowledge sources and multimedia alternatives to the textbook (Dede, 1998).

Students must not only know how to access the wide variety of information that technology affords us, they must also be able to process that information (Uchida et al, 1996).

Databases and computer technology are essential for involving students in locating pertinent information and resources and using them to conduct research, to problem solve, and to find answers to real-life questions (Darling-Hammond, 1994).

STRATEGIC ACTIVITIES

Objective: Use technological and informational resources to gather and synthesize information

Brainstorming and Discussion

- Have students work together to brainstorm all of the technological and information resources available to them that can be used to gather and synthesize information for a paper or project. Have students keep the list current to be used throughout the year as a resource.

Drawing and Artwork

- Have students use the computer to make graphic designs that will accompany a project or report they will submit.

Metaphors, Analogies, and Similes

- Encourage higher-level thinking by engaging students with the following simile: A computer is like _____ because it _____. For example, students could say the following: *The computer is like a filing cabinet because it stores information.*

Music, Rhythm, Rhyme, and Rap

- Have students download music (from legitimate sources) from the Internet and incorporate it into a PowerPoint presentation to enhance the quality of the content.

- Access music from the Internet to play for students. Use classical, jazz, new age, and other types of calming music to relieve anger and stress and prepare students' brains to learn. To create an energetic and upbeat mood, play music with a faster tempo that gets students excited about learning, such as the theme from *Rocky* or "Celebrate" by Kool and the Gang.

Project-Based and Problem-Based Instruction

- Require that students have between 5 and 10 different references for a paper or project. The references should represent at least four sources of information such as the following: Web sites, newspapers, books, and periodicals.

Reciprocal Teaching and Cooperative Learning

- Engage students in online discussions with students around the globe regarding a topic of interest.

Technology

- Appropriate computer programs can be used to teach phonemic analysis and other pertinent reading skills.

- Involve students in WISE (Web-based Integrated Science Environment) projects by accessing the following Web site: http://wise.berkeley.edu. Select activities from the project library that connect students to their curriculum. The WISE curriculum uses scientific models and connects them to problems that are personally relevant, such as space exploration, environmental stewardship, or wilderness survival. For example, in the "Houses in the Desert" project, students work with a partner to design a house that would be suitable for living in the desert (Linn & Slotta, 2000).

- Teach students to e-mail and then have them correspond via e-mail with other students in distant locations. Insist that students' e-mails be clearly written and grammatically correct.

- Teach students how to locate information for a paper or project by accessing the Internet and the World Wide Web.

- Have students do an ERIC search to locate information that can be used to research a given topic. Students must cite sources for the information they find.

- Engage students in video conferencing with other students around the world.

Visuals

- Have students integrate video clips into PowerPoint presentations to enhance the appeal of their presentations.

- Utilize video clips to illustrate important points to be made in a lesson. Show segments of videos that portray historical events or movie versions of books to be read. Have students compare and contrast the textbook version with the video. For example, when teaching Shakespeare's *Romeo and Juliet*, have students watch segments of *West Side Story*, an updated version of *Romeo and Juliet* in which the feud takes place between two rival New York street gangs, the Jets and the Sharks.

- Create an environmental print wall, actually a word wall, that exposes students to a type of environmental print—either general print, such as *Words in Our Surroundings*, or specific categories of print, such as *Cereal We Eat* or *Clothes We Wear*. Have students bring in examples to be placed on the wall as they continually increase their vocabularies.

Writing and Journals

- Have students use a word processing program to produce a research paper or other type of writing. Teach them to use all aspects of the computer program, such as making changes in the text by cutting and pasting.

REFLECTION AND APPLICATION

> ## Which strategies can I use to engage students' brains in using technological and informational resources?

Standard/Objective: _____

_____

_____.

Activity: _____

_____

_____.

Standard/Objective: _____

_____

_____.

Activity: _____

_____

_____.

Standard/Objective: _____

_____

_____.

Activity: _____

_____

_____.

Standard/Objective: _____

_____

_____.

Activity: _____

_____

_____.

14

Respecting Diversity in Language

American educators must make certain that the curriculum is inclusive of books that represent cultures other than the mainstream.

—Yokota, 1993

I spent nearly 30 years working with a school system so diverse that in some schools a mini United Nations existed. As many as 40 languages were spoken at Woodward Elementary, Sequoyah Middle, and Cross Keys High School in the DeKalb County School System near Atlanta, Georgia. These schools were places where diversity was not just tolerated but valued and celebrated and where a great deal of learning took place that was not necessarily written in any teacher's lesson plans.

Research has shown that when students' cultural, ethnic, and dialectal differences are recognized and used as springboards for teaching, all students benefit. Multicultural readers bring to the text a wide variety of real-world experiences, and, with discourse, these experiences and the prior knowledge derived from them provide the context for comprehension (Anderson & Barnitz, 1984). In fact, all students are more engaged and successful if the reading material relates to them and directly matches their cultural background. If students are reading text that is culturally unfamiliar, teachers must provide the context and schemata to support an understanding of the background and text structure so necessary for comprehension. The activities that follow will help in this regard.

RELEVANT RESEARCH

Students develop an understanding of respect for diversity in language use, patterns, and dialects across cultures, ethnic groups, geographic regions, and social roles (NCTE/IRA, 1996, Standard IX).

When teachers respect the diverse dialects of their students, they strengthen the process of teaching speakers of other languages to read standard English (Barnitz, 1994).

American educators must make certain that the curriculum is inclusive of books that represent cultures other than the mainstream (Yokota, 1993).

The following criteria should be used in selecting multicultural literature: (1) the literature is culturally accurate and reflects the beliefs and values of the culture; (2) details from the culture are a natural part of the story line; (3) the dialogue and relationships in the text are authentic; (4) cultural issues are portrayed realistically and in enough detail to inform the reader; and (5) characters are unique individuals whose lives are reflected in the culture, not merely included simply as representative of the minority (Yokota, 1993).

The experience-text-relationship (ETR) method enables learners to construct meaning by connecting the unique knowledge of their culture with any text (Au, 1993).

Quality multicultural literature should depict experiences that are historically authentic and aesthetic in nature (Harris, 1990).

When teachers construct semantic maps on the board, they provide multicultural students with visual ways of planning compositions because maps enable them to connect the major and minor ideas in their compositions (Sinatra, Beaudry, Stahl-Gemake, & Guastello, 1990).

A five-phase model for studying multicultural literature encompasses the following: (1) read folktales, fables, myths, and legends from one particular cultural group, such as Native Americans; (2) narrow the reading to folktales, myths, or legends from one or two cultural areas, such as Native Americans of the Southwest pueblos; (3) move to autobiographies, biographies, or informational text; (4) proceed to historical fiction; and (5) finish with modern realistic fiction, poetry, or biography written by authors of the specific cultural group who write for children (Norton, 1990).

Students have a difficult time retaining information that is not connected to their lives and personal experiences (Hansen & Hubbard, 1984).

Students from lower socioeconomic backgrounds often have a difficult time organizing their writing because they have little knowledge of the form and structure of standard English (Chall & Jacobs, 1983).

STRATEGIC ACTIVITIES

*Objective: Respect diversity
in language use, patterns, and dialects*

Brainstorming and Discussion

• Find literary selections where the same story is told from several multicultural perspectives. Have students discuss the similarities and differences in the plot of the respective stories. For example, compare the original story of Cinderella to the African folktale *Mufaro's Beautiful Daughters* by John Steptoe.

• Provide time each week for students to conduct book talks in which they give a brief summary of multicultural books they have read and whether they would recommend that book to other students.

Drawing and Artwork

• Imitating characteristics of another culture's artwork enables a student to gain insight into that culture. Engage students in a class discussion regarding the ideas and feelings a culture communicates through its artwork. Then have students imitate that art form by making original drawings or paintings to illustrate their understanding of cultural characteristics.

Graphic Organizers, Semantic Maps, and Word Webs

• As stories are read and discussed, design graphic organizers on the board or an overhead to demonstrate to all students the connections between the major and minor ideas in the story. This activity is particularly beneficial for students for whom English is not a first language.

Humor

• Young and Ferguson (1998) composed an extensive list of what they call multicultural trickster tales in which characters use pranks, lies, and mischief to outwit more powerful characters. Have students enjoy these humorous stories as they learn about various cultures. An extensive list of trickster stories from a variety of cultures is included in the Young and Ferguson article.

Metaphors, Analogies, and Similes

• Have students find traits of two or more multicultural characters that are similar in some regard. Have them make comparisons and contrasts between the two characters.

- Have students compare a word in the English language to a comparable word in another language. For example, the French word *rouge,* meaning red, is the same word English speakers use for the colored makeup a woman wears on her cheeks.

Music, Rhythm, Rhyme, and Rap

- Bring in musical selections representative of a variety of cultures, such as salsa music from the Hispanic culture or a flute selection from Native American culture. As students listen to the music, have them discuss characteristics of the culture depicted in the music.

Storytelling

- Ensure that the curriculum and the classroom library include books that represent cultures other than those considered mainstream. Have students vary their independent reading selections to include a variety of multicultural selections.

- Have students read or use read-alouds from the extensive annotated list of multicultural literature contained in Junko Yokota's article "Issues in Selecting Multicultural Children's Literature" (1993).

Technology

- Have students use the computer to type a summary paragraph of a multicultural book they have read. Place the summary paragraphs on index cards and catalog them in a computerized file so that other students have access to a variety of annotated reading selections.

Visualization and Guided Imagery

- Following the reading of a multicultural piece of literature, have students visualize themselves living in that culture. Have them discuss how they would deal with authentic experiences or conflicts presented in the story. For example, ask students how they would have responded if they had been Anne Frank, the 13-year-old Jewish girl who hid in an attic above a warehouse in fear of being discovered by the German gestapo and sent to a concentration camp during World War II.

Visuals

- Have students work in pairs or small groups to develop photographic essays around a chosen topic or theme. Have students select a topic or theme such as *A Day in My Life.* Have them organize the theme into subheadings. Using a disposable camera, have students take pictures related to the theme. After picture development, have them organize and storyboard their pictures according to the headings and subheadings. Finally, while looking at the visual storyboard, have students write a composition on the topic in the order indicated on the storyboard (Sinatra et al., 1990).

REFLECTION AND APPLICATION

> ## Which strategies can I use to engage students' brains so that they respect diversity in language?

Standard/Objective: _____

_____

_____.

Activity: _____

_____

_____.

Standard/Objective: _____

_____

_____.

Activity: _____

_____

_____.

Standard/Objective: _____

_____

_____.

Activity: _____

_____

_____.

Standard/Objective: _____

_____

_____.

Activity: _____

_____

_____.

Standard/Objective: _____

_____

_____.

Activity: _____

_____

_____.

15

Developing Competency in English

Differences among students should not be seen as barriers to acquiring literacy.

—Strickland, 1998

My husband and I celebrated our 25th wedding anniversary with a cruise to the Hawaiian Islands. While on one of the islands, we took a tour that enabled us to appreciate fully the rich beauty and majesty of our 50th state. It is amazing how much knowledge can be gleaned from a field trip. That shouldn't have been a surprise to me, because taking field trips is one of the 20 brain-compatible strategies referred to in this book. But I digress.

One of the fascinating things we learned from our knowledgeable and humorous driver was the fact that the entire Hawaiian language is constituted of all of the vowels but only seven of the consonants from the English language. We learned that if a word contains any letters other than those seven included in the language, it is not truly a Hawaiian term. Wouldn't it be important for a teacher of diverse students to know this information if one of those students happened to speak Hawaiian? Wouldn't it be crucial for that teacher to make comparisons or connections between any new information being taught and the conceptual framework in the minds of students whose first language is not English?

RELEVANT RESEARCH

Students whose first language is not English make use of their language to develop competency in the English language arts and to develop understanding of content across the curriculum (NCTE/ IRA, 1996, Standard X).

Although a new language can be acquired at any age, the first five years appear optimal for language acquisition (Dhority & Jensen, 1998).

Language fluency is strengthened or weakened with intervention in the first two years of life (Dhority & Jensen, 1998).

Every child has cognitive and linguistic strategies despite what their first language may be or the socioeconomic level from which they come (Strickland, 1998).

Differences among students should not be seen as barriers to acquiring literacy (Strickland, 1998).

It could take five to seven years for students who are limited English speakers to gain enough skill with the language to perform successfully academically (Sutton, 1998).

Teachers can use the following seven strategies to create a classroom climate that promotes positive intercultural interactions: (1) build trust between teacher and student, (2) become literate concerning the specific culture(s) represented by the students, (3) build a repertoire of strategies for instruction, (4) use effective techniques to ask questions, (5) provide effective student feedback, (6) assess instructional materials for cultural sensitivity, and (7) establish positive relationships between home and school (Jackson, 1998).

Even adults stand a better chance of learning a second language when they are immersed in the vocabulary and context of the culture (Dhority & Jensen, 1998).

Putting too much emphasis on word attack skills or phonics drills in isolation may interfere with the students' ability to integrate language, print, and thinking (Sutton, 1998).

The *deficit theory* of language presupposes the superiority of standard English over other forms of language (Powell, 1998).

Students from diverse backgrounds will comprehend text poorly unless strategies are used that enable them to connect the text with their personal cultural and linguistic experiences (Barnitz, 1994).

Upon entrance to school, all children are highly competent in their use of language but they may not be in circumstances where they can demonstrate that competence (Cazden, 1988).

When English-speaking students are tutoring their ESL (English as a second language) buddies, they should use gestures and the strategies of role play, drawing, and the use of props, if necessary (Buehler & Meltesen, 1983).

STRATEGIC ACTIVITIES

Objective: ESL students use first language to develop competency in English

Brainstorming and Discussion

• Following the introduction of a key vocabulary concept, have students whose first language is not English discuss with a partner or the entire class the pronunciation of a word in their language that has the same or a similar meaning to the key concept being taught.

• Before reading narrative or expository texts, spend time engaging students (whose first language is not standard English) in a discussion that will build the necessary background to understand the major concepts in the text.

• Always establish a purpose for students to read both narrative or expository texts. This will assist ESL students with comprehension of unfamiliar texts because it will direct their attention to specific key concepts.

• Ask higher-level questions of students that encourage them to make predictions, draw conclusions, or compare and contrast in their discussions. For example, *What do you think will happen next?* or *How does this story compare with the one we read the other day?*

Drawing and Artwork

• Have students whose first language is not English illustrate a key vocabulary word to assist them in comprehending the definition. Underneath the illustration, have students write the English word and the corresponding word in their native language.

Games

• Have students play any of the games listed in Chapter 4, "Vocabulary Instruction," to increase all students' knowledge of the English language. Assign a student who is fluent in English to play these games with any student whose first language is not English. This way, the nonnative English speaker has assistance when needed.

Humor

• Have students work in cooperative groups to write riddles or jokes involving the content or story discussed. Have them share their efforts with the class.

Metaphors, Analogies, and Similes

• Integrate any new information to be taught into students' existing knowledge by using the strategy of metaphor, analogy, and simile. For example, when a new word is introduced, try to make a comparison between this concept and one that may be in the students' native language.

Music, Rhythm, Rhyme, and Rap

• Have students work in cooperative groups to write a song, rhyme, or rap that will symbolize their understanding of a concept just taught.

Project-Based and Problem-Based Instruction

• Have students work individually or in groups to create word problems in mathematics or crossword puzzles in English that can be solved by their classmates.

• Involve students in projects that assist all students, even those who are not native English speakers, in integrating curricular objectives in a more authentic and meaningful context. Assign specific roles that enable all students to participate in meaningful ways. For example, an ESL student might be asked to provide the illustrations for the project until he or she feels comfortable functioning in a more verbal role.

Role Plays, Drama, Pantomimes, and Charades

• A concept called *Total Physical Response (TPR)* is effective for teaching vocabulary concepts to ESL students. This technique involves the use of body movement by having students act out key concepts that they are trying to learn in English. The use of the body not only provides a visual but also places the information in procedural memory, a strong memory system for the brain.

Visuals

• Have students explore the visuals in specific types of reading material to assist in making predictions and comprehending text. For example, teach students how to read chapter headings and subheadings, italicized or boldface printed words, charts, graphs, illustrations, or any other pertinent visuals in content-area texts.

REFLECTION AND APPLICATION

> ## Which strategies can I use to engage students' brains so that they develop competency in English?

Standard/Objective: _____
_____
_____.

Activity: _____
_____
_____.

Standard/Objective: _____
_____
_____.

Activity: _____
_____
_____.

Standard/Objective: _____
_____
_____.

Activity: _____
_____
_____.

Standard/Objective: _____
_____
_____.

Activity: _____
_____
_____.

Standard/Objective: _____
_____
_____.

Activity: _____
_____
_____.

16

Participating in Literacy Communities

The best literature discussion groups are student led.

—Scharer, 1992

Visualize the following elementary classroom. Students are seated at tables that facilitate their ability to talk and work together when necessary. In the middle of each table is a wicker basket where books for varying reading abilities are displayed. There is a classroom library stocked with books that are also at a variety of reading levels. Big Books are housed in a wooden case near the classroom library. Students are happily engaged in a variety of literacy experiences. Two children are quietly doing partner reading of a selection that will be read tomorrow. Some students are working on a revised draft of a piece of writing for publication. Others are reading words they see around the room, which is replete with labeled items and the walls displayed with student work. The teacher is conducting a guided reading lesson at the reading table. There is a comfortable rocking chair labeled "author's chair" where students sit to read work they have composed. This is a classroom where literacy is alive and well and students and teachers participate daily in a variety of literacy activities for different purposes.

Now visualize a middle or high school classroom. Is your vision much different? It shouldn't be. With the exception of some labeled items and perhaps a few Big Books, all students, regardless of their age or grade level, should participate in similar literacy communities.

RELEVANT RESEARCH

Students participate as knowledgeable, reflective, creative, and critical members of a variety of literacy communities (NCTE/IRA, 1996, Standard XI).

The Four Block format enables teachers to develop comprehending readers by addressing vocabulary development, guided reading, writing, and independent reading all in a 60- to 90-minute time period (Chapman & King, 2003).

Programs such as *Junior Great Books, National Writing Project, Project Success Enrichment,* and the *Exemplary Center for Reading Instruction* are all included in an analysis of seven programs that work to improve literacy in the middle and high school grades (Killion, 2003).

Cooperative literature discussion groups promote the learning of new vocabulary in context because students can select the new words to be learned (Blachowicz & Fisher, 2002).

Asking questions that cause students to reflect can double the number of facts and concepts learned during a lesson (Gibbs, 2001).

Teachers should ask the following three types of reflective questions during an academic lesson: (1) content-thinking questions that concentrate on the facts and concepts needed to work with the content, (2) collaborative-social questions that concentrate on the interactions and social skills used during the completion of the activity, and (3) personal learning questions that concentrate on what an individual student has learned or how that student has felt during the activity (Gibbs, 2001).

Student-led literacy conferences enable parents to understand what their child is learning because the child explains what is contained in their portfolios (Routman, 2000).

When students are involved in a Socratic seminar, a discussion strategy used following the reading of a selection, they are able to use student dialogue to construct knowledge (Tanner & Cassados, 1998).

The best literature discussion groups are student-led in which questioning is higher level and questions are open-ended and in which students have a voice (Scharer, 1992).

Having students keep literature logs develops sight vocabulary in the primary grades and meaning vocabulary in the upper grades (Atwell, 1987).

Quality questions challenge the thought processes of the brain (Berliner, 1984).

Students remember 90% of what they teach to others (Dale, 1969; Sousa, 1995).

STRATEGIC ACTIVITIES

Objective: Participate in a variety of literacy communities

Brainstorming and Discussion

• Give students a question to which there may be more than one answer. Have students participate in a brainstorming session, deriving multiple ideas while ensuring that they follow *DOVE* guidelines, which are as follows:

Students *Defer* judgment when other students are contributing.

Students give only *One* idea at a time.

Students are encouraged to give a *Variety* of ideas.

Students direct their *Energy* to the task at hand.

• Have students form small groups called literature circles. All students read the same story, poem, or book and engage in a discussion of that selection with members of the group assigned specific roles to perform. Some possible roles are as follows:

Discussion Director. Formulates the questions to be discussed and makes sure that all group members contribute

Literary Luminary. Reads orally the most important parts of the text

Connector. Assists group in connecting ideas in the real world with the text read

Illustrator. Draws pictures for clarification

Summarizer. Periodically highlights the main ideas of the discussion

Vocabulary Enricher. Provides definitions for any unfamiliar words that are crucial to understanding the text

Investigator. Supplies any necessary background information the group needs

SOURCE: Adapted from Vacca et al., 2003.

• Involve students in a Socratic seminar by following the procedure outlined below:

1. Determine the main idea from a book, story, or poem previously read.

2. Design a series of questions that encourage students to think at the application, analysis, synthesis, and evaluation levels of Bloom's taxonomy.

3. Have students who will be participating in the discussion sit in an inner circle. Sit students who will be taking notes in the outer circle.

4. Begin a 10–15 minute discussion by asking a core question in the series of questions. Continue to engage students by asking additional questions.

5. Have a student in the inner or outer circle summarize the main points made during the discussion.

6. Debrief with students by asking for ways in which the seminar could have been improved. Implement any meaningful suggestions during the next seminar (Tanner & Cassados, 1998).

• Before, during, and after the completion of a reading or language arts activity, have students reflect on the three types of questions described in the research section of this chapter. The first type of questions relate to the content of the task. For example, in the book *Hatchet* by Gary Paulsen, *What was the first thing Brian did when he discovered that he was all alone in the wilderness?* The second round of questions should focus on the social interactions experienced by the group, such as *Did everyone have an opportunity to participate in our discussion of the story?* The third type of questioning deals with the students' personal involvement with the text, such as *If you had been stranded in the wilderness like Brian, what would you have done?*

Drawing and Artwork

• Provide students with a variety of opportunities to demonstrate their understanding of a literary selection read. They might choose to design a cartoon showing the sequence of events in a story, draw a book jacket that illustrates the main idea of a poem or story, or assemble a collage depicting the significant details in a story.

Music, Rhythm, Rhyme, and Rap

• Have students work in cooperative groups to write a song, rhyme, or rap symbolizing their knowledge of a literary work they have read. Students then share their creative effort with the remainder of the class and are assessed according to a rubric that all students helped to develop. The rubric could include the following dimensions: includes at least five major details from the literary work, is performed with enthusiasm, and shows creative effort.

Project-Based and Problem-Based Instruction

• Have students participate in meaningful literacy lessons through the Four-Block planning model. Divide a 60- to 90-minute block of time into the following four blocks: vocabulary development, guided reading, writing, and independent reading. Part of each block is devoted to a teacher-directed lesson. During the remainder of each block, students may participate in total group activities, working alone, with a partner, or individually participating in literacy activities designed to address specific objectives. For example, in the vocabulary development block, students work in small groups to role play vocabulary words. In the guided reading block, the teacher provides a lesson on identifying main idea by comparing it to the top of a table and the supporting details to the legs of the table. During the writing block, students write a composition in which every paragraph contains a main idea sentence. Finally, in the independent reading block, students read books that contain an obvious main idea, such as *The Important Book* by Margaret Wise Brown.

• Have students participate in a variety of opportunities that are included in a listing of the seven research-based programs that appear to work in increasing literacy for middle and high school students. (Refer to the research section of this chapter.) These include but are not limited to *Junior Great Books, National Writing Project, Project Success Enrichment,* and the *6 + 1 Trait Writing Model.*

• Have students participate in a variety of opportunities to read independently. Such programs as *SSR (Self-sustained Silent Reading)* and *DEAR (Drop Everything and Read)* enable students to spend quality time reading silently, just as lifelong readers do. The more time students spend in authentic reading tasks, the better readers they become.

Storytelling

• Provide opportunities for students to share their literary experiences with one another. Allow time for students to share a summary and their opinion of a book read with the entire class or a small group. Students could then engage in a book exchange and read one another's books.

Writing and Journals

• Have students sit in the "author's chair" when reading a piece of original writing to classmates. This simple but meaningful procedure builds confidence in students as they are able to share their best thoughts with peers.

REFLECTION AND APPLICATION

> ## Which strategies can I use to engage students' brains as they participate in literacy communities?

Standard/Objective: _____
_____
_____.

Activity: _____
_____
_____.

Standard/Objective: _____
_____
_____.

Activity: _____
_____
_____.

Standard/Objective: _____
_____
_____.

Activity: _____
_____
_____.

Standard/Objective: _____
_____
_____.

Activity: _____
_____
_____.

Standard/Objective: _____
_____
_____.

Activity: _____
_____
_____.

17

Using Language to Accomplish Purposes

Tell me, I forget.

Show me, I remember.

Involve me, I understand.

—Ancient Chinese proverb

Learning style theorists know that the more modalities a teacher uses in engaging students, the more likely it is that the information will be understood and retained. This is why we only remember 10% of what we hear, 20% of what we see, 30% of what we see and hear, and as much as 90% of what we say or discuss as we teach others (Sousa, 1995). In fact, one of the most promising features of the 20 brain-compatible strategies delineated in this book is the fact that by the time you have used all 20 strategies, you have taught to all four modalities—visual, auditory, tactile, and kinesthetic—several times over (see Figure 1 in the Introduction). Research (Gardner, 1983; McCarthy, 1990) also indicates that the more modalities a teacher uses to input information into the brain, the more channels the brain has for accessing the information. Therefore, when students are taught to use spoken (auditory), written (tactile), and visual language for distinct purposes, learning is enhanced.

Having students use a variety of genres to express themselves broadens the options for learning, makes teaching more enjoyable, and equips students with exciting and novel cross-curricular ways to communicate. Furthermore, when students use a variety of modalities and genres to accomplish their own individual purposes, it increases the likelihood of their becoming lifelong learners.

RELEVANT RESEARCH

Students use spoken, written, and visual language to accomplish their own purposes (e.g., for learning, enjoyment, persuasion, and the exchange of information) (NCTE/IRA, 1996, Standard XII).

Eventually students are capable of reading and writing words that are more advanced than those in their speaking vocabularies (Wolfe & Nevills, 2004).

Select materials for read-alouds to students that are several levels higher than the students' own reading levels (Wolfe & Nevills, 2004).

Competent readers learn more vocabulary through exposure to print than to exposure to conversation (Wolfe & Nevills, 2004).

A students' reading vocabulary does not approximate the oral vocabulary until seventh or eighth grade (Biemiller, 2003).

Humor makes everyday information come alive because it increases retention, relieves stress, and lessens tension for adults as well as students (Chapman & King, 2003).

Every genre presents a new and different way to record and remember the information being learned (Chapman & King, 2003).

When visual images such as vivid illustrations are present, children often ignore the print and depend on the pictures to help them answer comprehension questions (Beck & McKeown, 2001).

Students' writing should reflect the same real-world authenticity as adult writing, even within the parameters of required standards and curriculum (Atwell, 1987).

When students utilize various genres, they experience different ways to communicate through writing (Atwell, 1987).

Oral language activities are great ways to encourage students to make predictions regarding the use of words in a story to be read (Duffelmeyer, 1980).

STRATEGIC ACTIVITIES

Objective: Use spoken, written, and visual language to accomplish purposes

Drawing and Artwork

• Have students design a poster as a visual to show what they learned following the teaching of a chapter or unit of study. For example, after a study of the planets, students design a poster on which they draw a picture of a selected planet and write the five most important facts to remember about it.

Humor

• Have students create cartoons or comic strips based on the information gleaned in a unit of study. When students become comfortable with this medium, they may want to tackle editorial cartoons that involve the use of higher-level thinking skills and show a students' point of view.

• Have students create riddles and jokes based on the information derived from a chapter or unit of study.

Project-Based and Problem-Based Instruction

• Have students select a topic and complete a science project that adheres to the steps in the scientific process including the following: statement of the problem, hypothesis, methodology, conclusions. Students write a paper delineating a detailed description of the steps in the process, create an attractive backboard as a visual, and plan an oral presentation to a panel of judges describing the implementation of the project.

• Have students interview a family member or a close friend and then, based on the information gleaned from the interview, write the biography of the person interviewed. I will always remember having to interview my mother for a graduate class assignment. I learned things about her life that I would not have learned otherwise.

• Create an authentic project that addresses several content-area objectives. For example, have students write and produce a news show that would address curricular objectives within a real-world context. Students would research contemporary or historical events to determine which stories are important enough to be included in the broadcast, write the news copy being sure that the copy is grammatically correct, and actually prepare to broadcast the news using the most appropriate on-camera public speaking skills (Tate, 2003).

• Have students produce and broadcast a school news program that airs daily over the closed-circuit television in the school. Students write copy about the important events happening in the school community, tell the lunch menu and the food groups to which those lunch items belong, or recommend a good book for independent reading. They can take turns as anchor people who broadcast the news.

Role Plays, Drama, Pantomimes, and Charades

• Have students put a storybook character or historical figure on trial. For example, John Wilkes Booth could be put on trial for the assassination of President Abraham Lincoln. Actual story or historical events constitute the evidence. Have specific students play the parts of the prosecuting or defense attorneys as well as the judge and jury. Following the role play of the trial, the jury decides the fate of the person on trial based on the evidence presented and the presentation skills of the attorneys.

Technology

- Have students produce a PowerPoint presentation to demonstrate what they have learned following the teaching of a chapter or unit of study. For example, following a study of the Revolutionary or Civil War, students' PowerPoint presentation is designed to visually display important details regarding the war including the causes, significant battles, heroes, and so forth.

- Have students write an e-mail to a friend. Have them write the e-mail in a clear and concise way, limiting the information to only the most important details.

Writing and Journals

- Have students write a letter to the editor regarding a topic of interest or current event. Have them express an opinion and include facts to support that opinion. Students read aloud their editorials in an effort to convince classmates of their point of view.

- Have students write in personal journals regarding topics of choice, including reflections on class assignments and personal thoughts or feelings. Journals are typically not graded but provide a valuable outlet for purposeful writing and the written expression of emotions.

REFLECTION AND APPLICATION

> **Which strategies can I use to
> engage students' brains as they
> use language for their own purposes?**

Standard/Objective: _____

_____

_____.

Activity: _____

_____

_____.

Standard/Objective: _____

_____

_____.

Activity: _____

_____

_____.

Standard/Objective: _____

_____

_____.

Activity: _____

_____

_____.

Standard/Objective: _____

_____

_____.

Activity: _____

_____

_____.

Standard/Objective: _____

_____

_____.

Activity: _____

_____

_____.

Resource

Brain-Compatible Lesson Planning

Some teachers write out their lesson plans in an appropriate book designated for that purpose. Other teachers use online resources for planning and recording the intent of lesson delivery. Regardless of the lesson-planning format you use, there are five questions you should keep in the forefront of your mind when planning a reading or language arts lesson that will truly be brain-compatible. Those five questions are provided and explained on the pages that follow.

QUESTION 1: WHAT READING OR LANGUAGE ARTS OBJECTIVE(S) WILL YOU BE TEACHING? ■

Obviously, the first question any teacher should ask is *What am I getting ready to teach?* In other words, *What is the purpose of my lesson?* This is not a teacher's decision to make. Teacher's teach what is designated by national, state, and local standards and curricular objectives. They teach what has been mandated by standardized and criterion-referenced tests. In fact, there are so many skills and objectives in the reading and language arts curriculum that teachers would be wise to consider which objectives deserve more time and attention than others. They must consider which objectives will contribute to increased literacy for the students.

They must also consider for which standards or objectives students will be held accountable on mandated measures of accountability. You can be the most brain-compatible instructor on earth, but if the skills and objectives that are tested are not the ones that you have taught, then *Houston, we have a major problem.* Your exceptional teaching will not be reflected in the test scores of your students. Nothing destroys students' confidence more quickly than to look at a reading or language arts test item and realize that they do not even begin to know how to address that item because the content was never taught, or perhaps never learned. If there are 10 questions on the test that ask students to tell the main idea of a story, then you will definitely want to spend quality time on main idea. Besides, it's an important skill, so the time is time well spent!

So what is the answer to the first question? You will be teaching every tested objective and more. There is so much that students need to know that is never formally assessed. Teach it anyway! You are producing literate, lifelong readers, not just proficient test takers. We all know what happens when students simply cram for the exam. They forget the information immediately after they take it. Teach so that your students acquire the love of reading. After all, those who don't read are no more literate than those who cannot.

■ QUESTION 2: HOW WILL YOU KNOW THAT STUDENTS HAVE LEARNED THE CONTENT OR ACQUIRED THE SKILL?

I am a Covey trainer for the *7 Habits of Highly Effective People.* Habit Number 2 simply states, *Begin with the end in mind.* This statement could never be truer than when it comes to assessment. Question 2 involves visualizing what students should know and be able to do at the culmination of your reading and language arts lesson, then working backward to help them achieve the visualization. If you don't know what you expect from students, then don't expect to get it.

It is also crucially important that if the objective you are teaching is one that is also tested, students must be exposed to the same format in which they will see this objective on the test. Let's take main idea as our example. As a reading specialist, I have taught the concept of main idea many times. I usually teach it using the strategy of **metaphor, analogy, and simile.** I tell my students that the main idea in a passage or story is like the top of a table and the supporting details in the passage are like the legs of the table. Just like the legs hold up the table, so the supporting details hold up the main idea. Students always understood this concept, especially because we drew a table on our papers and wrote the main idea of the passage on the top of the table and one supporting detail on each of the legs. I now know, however, that if I want my students to get all of the main idea questions correct on the test, I have to take them one step further. I have to teach them the format of the test. I have to give them examples of ways in which main idea is tested. I have to let them know that they will be asked to read a passage and select either the main idea of the story from four answer choices or they will be asked to select the best title for the story from four answer choices. They may also be asked for the theme of the story. Students need to understand that theme also relates to main idea.

Once I had taught each skill using the brain-compatible strategies in this book and we have practiced one or two formatted test items, my students were always confident that they could knock the top off the test. Yours will be, too.

QUESTION 3: HOW WILL YOU GAIN AND MAINTAIN YOUR STUDENTS' ATTENTION?

A brain concept called the theory of *primacy and recency* states that the brain pays closest attention to the first thing it hears in a learning segment and pays second closest attention to the last thing it hears. It stands to reason that the middle of a learning segment, movie, or even a television show will be least remembered. Therefore, it would be wise for teachers to spend time at the beginning of a lesson engaging students' brains or hooking them into the lesson. Teachers would also do well to spend time at the end of a lesson reviewing what has been taught so that the last thing the student hears remains memorable. If a teacher teaches in segments or chunks of information, there are multiple beginnings and endings (*primacies and recencies)* in a class period or a reading block.

Because the beginning of the lesson is the most remembered, then time spent engaging students' brains or hooking them into the lesson is time well spent. Brain research also tells us that there are four basic ways to engage students' brains: *need, novelty, meaning,* and *emotion.* Each way is briefly described in the paragraphs that follow.

Every brain learns what it needs to know or what it has a purpose to learn. Therefore, one way to engage students is to tell them what they will be learning and why they need to know it. If you cannot think of a reason to teach a specific objective, why should you waste time teaching it? In our main idea example, we could use need by telling students that good readers and writers often need only to get the gist or most important major ideas of a passage, newspaper article, or story.

Novelty is the second way to gain students' attention. The brain pays attention to things that are new or different. If you teach your students in a variety of ways and through a variety of modalities, students will pay attention. There are multiple ways to teach main idea contained in this book. Select the ones that you think are most appropriate for your students.

To make anything meaningful to the brain, teachers must find ways to connect the information to their real, authentic lives. One question each teacher should ask is *How can I relate this reading or language arts concept to my students' lives?* If you can think of a way, then use meaning to gain students' attention for the lesson.

The final way to gain attention is through emotion. Of all of the ways, this is the most powerful. The brain seldom forget events with an emotional connection. Ask yourself what you were doing when you heard in 1986 that the *Challenger* had exploded with a teacher on board. You probably remember exactly what you were doing at the time. When teachers share stories that are emotional, when they are passionate about good literature, that passion becomes contagious.

■ QUESTION 4: HOW WILL YOU CHUNK THE CONTENT TO ENGAGE THE BRAINS OF YOUR STUDENTS?

I believe it was Madeline Hunter who asked the following question: *How do you eat an elephant?* The answer was always *One bite at a time.* Brain research teaches us that our brains can only hold a limited number of isolated items in short-term memory at one time. Seven items is the average for most people aged 15 years and older. It is less for younger students. If I give you any more items to remember simultaneously than the number of items your brain can hold, it will not remember the additional items. It's like marbles in a jar. When the jar is full, putting in any more marbles will cause some to fall out.

This is the reason so much in the world comes in a series of seven—seven days in a week, seven digits in a phone number, seven continents, seven colors in the rainbow, seven notes on the scale, Seven Seas, Seven Wonders of the Ancient World, Seven Dwarfs, *7 Habits of Highly Effective People,* seven initial multiple intelligences. You get the idea! If you want the adult brain to hold more than seven items, then you must find a way to chunk the information together so that it is not taught in isolation. An example would be your social security number. Because it consists of more than seven digits, it is divided into three chunks to make it easier for you to remember. In fact, the brain can remember a chunk as if it were a single item.

What are the implications of this fact on your lesson planning? Now that you know your students' brains can hold only a limited number of isolated items, it would behoove you to find ways to divide the content into meaningful chunks and connect those chunks together so that your students' brains can retain more information. For example, if you know that an 11-year-old can typically hold only five isolated bits of information, why teach him 10 vocabulary words at one time? If you do teach 10, then find a way to connect all of them together through a story or a role play, or teach five words and the synonyms or antonyms for those same words.

■ QUESTION 5: HOW DID YOU INTEGRATE THE 20 STRATEGIES INTO YOUR LESSON DESIGN AND DELIVERY?

As you plan your lessons, keep this book and the following list of the 20 strategies close at hand. When you have finished, see how many of the 20 strategies listed were actually incorporated into your lesson. If the answer is none of them, then stop—go back and plan it again! Why would you want to teach reading and language arts without taking advantage of the ways in which your students' brains learn? Teaching is hard work. Teachers need to teach smarter, not harder! Teaching smarter means teaching in ways that go along with the way the brain learns, which means incorporating the following strategies into your lesson plans:

1. Brainstorming and Discussion

2. Drawing and Artwork

3. Field Trips

4. Games

5. Graphic Organizers, Semantic Maps, and Word Webs

6. Humor

7. Manipulatives

8. Metaphors, Analogies, and Similes

9. Mnemonic Devices

10. Movement

11. Music, Rhythm, Rhyme, and Rap

12. Project-Based and Problem-Based Instruction

13. Reciprocal Teaching and Cooperative Learning

14. Role Plays, Drama, Pantomimes, and Charades

15. Storytelling

16. Technology

17. Visualization and Guided Imagery

18. Visuals

19. Work Study and Apprenticeships

20. Writing and Journals

There is no magic number of strategies to be used in one lesson. Because you know that you have students of all four modalities in any class, however, always attempt to incorporate at least one visual, one auditory, one tactile, and one kinesthetic strategy into every lesson. See Figure 1 in the Introduction for a correlation of the 20 strategies to the multiple intelligences and the learning modalities.

Let's go back to our main idea example. By the time I have completed my teaching of the concept of main idea, we could have used the simile comparing the main idea to a table, we could have drawn the table (tactile), we could have worked with a partner to discuss the main idea of a given passage or story (auditory), we could have drawn the graphic organizer found in Chapter 5, "Text Comprehension Instruction," to demonstrate how the details add up to the main idea (visual), and we could have taken several sets of main ideas and details, placed them on cards, randomly assigned them to students, and had students come to the front of the room and arrange themselves so that the appropriate main idea is adjacent to the supporting details (kinesthetic). By the time we finished this multiple-day lesson, students would truly understand the concept of main idea. I would only need to do one more thing: Allow students to practice several sample or benchmark items that show how main idea is tested.

By following this plan, not only would students have the confidence to knock the top off the test, they would also spend a lifetime comprehending the main idea in authentic contexts.

Bibliography

Adams, M. J., Foorman, B. R., Lundberg, I., & Beeler, T. (1998). *Phonemic awareness in young children. A classroom curriculum.* Baltimore: Brookes.

Allington, R. L. (1984). Content coverage and contextual reading in reading groups. *Journal of Reading Behavior, 26,* 85–96.

Anderson, S. (2004). *The book of reading and writing: Ideas, tips, and lists for the elementary classroom.* Thousand Oaks, CA: Corwin Press.

Anderson, B. V., & Barnitz, J. G. (1984). Cross-cultural schemata and reading comprehension instruction. In M. F. Opitz (Ed.), *Literacy instruction for culturally and linguistically diverse students* (pp. 95–101). Newark, DE: International Reading Association.

Anderson, R. C., Wilson, P. T., & Fielding, L. G. (1988, Summer). Growth in reading and how children spend their time outside of school. *Reading Research Quarterly,* 285–303.

Andrews, K., & Marshall, K. (2000). Making learning connections through telelearning. *Educational Leadership, 58,* 53–56.

Atwell, N. (1987). *In the middle: Writing, reading, and learning with adolescents.* Portsmouth, NH: Boynton/Cook.

Au, K. (1993). *Literacy instruction in multicultural settings.* Fort Worth, TX. Harcourt Brace.

Au, K. (1994). Issue. *ASCD Update, 36*(5), 7.

Baechtold, S., & Algiers, A. (1986). Teaching college students vocabulary with rhyme, rhythm, and ritzy characters. *Journal of Reading, 30,* 248–253.

Barnitz, J. G. (1994). Discourse diversity: Principles for authentic talk and literacy instruction. *Journal of Reading, 37,* 586–591.

Bayer, J. (1984). *A, my name is Alice.* New York: Dial Books for Young Readers.

Beck, I. L., & McKeown, M. G. (2001). Text talk: Capturing the benefits of read-aloud experiences for young children. *Reading Teacher, 55*(1), 10–21.

Bender, W. N. (2002). *Differentiating instruction for students with learning disabilities.* Thousand Oaks, CA: Corwin Press.

Bender, W. N. (2003). *Reading strategies for elementary students with learning difficulties.* Thousand Oaks, CA: Corwin Press.

Berliner, D. C. (1984). *The half-full glass: A review of research on teaching.* In P. L. Hosford (Ed.), *Using what we know about teaching* (pp. 511–577). Alexandria, VA: Association for Supervision and Curriculum Development.

Biemiller, A. (2003, May). *Using stories to promote vocabulary.* Paper presented at symposium, *Fostering early narrative competency: Innovations in instruction,* conducted by International Reading Association, Orlando, FL.

Blachowicz, C., & Fisher, P. J. (2002). *Teaching vocabulary in all classrooms* (2nd ed.). Upper Saddle River, NJ: Merrill Prentice Hall.

Brett, A., Rothlein, L., & Hurley, M. (1996). Vocabulary acquisition from listening to stories and explanations of target words. *Elementary School Journal, 96*(4), 415–422.

Buehler, E. C., & Meltesen, D. (1983). ESL buddies. *Instructor, 93*(2), 120–124.

Burgess, R. (2000). *Laughing lessons: 149 2/3 ways to make teaching and learning fun.* Minneapolis, MN: Free Spirit.

Buzan, T., & Buzan, B. (1994). *The mind map book.* New York: NAL-Dutton.

Caine, R. N., & Caine, G. (1994). *Making connections: Teaching and the human brain.* Menlo Park, CA: Addison-Wesley.

Calkins, L. M. (1994). *The art of teaching writing.* Portsmouth, NH: Heinemann.

Cardoso, S. H. (2000). Our ancient laughing brain. *Cerebrum: The Dana Forum on Brain Science, 2*(4).

Carter, R. (1998). *Mapping the mind.* Los Angeles: University of California Press.

Cazden, C. B. (1988). *Classroom discourse: The language of teaching and learning.* Portsmouth, NH: Heinemann.

Chall, J., & Jacobs, V. (1983). Writing and reading in elementary grades: Developmental trends among low SES children. *Language Arts, 60,* 617–626.

Chapman, C., & King, R. (2003). *Differentiated instructional strategies for reading in the content areas.* Thousand Oaks, CA. Corwin Press.

Clay, M. (1991). *Becoming literate: Construction of inner control.* Portsmouth, NH: Heinemann.

Clay, M. M. (1993). *Reading Recovery. A guidebook for teachers in training.* Portsmouth, NH: Heinemann.

College Board. (2000). *The College Board: Preparing, inspiring, and connecting.* Retrieved from www.collegeboard.org/

Dale, E. (1969). *Audio-visual methods in teaching* (3rd ed.). New York: Holt, Rinehart and Winston.

d'Anna, C. A., Zechmeister, E. B., & Hall, J. W. (1991). Toward a meaningful definition of vocabulary size. *Journal of Reading Behavior, 23,* 109–122.

Darling-Hammond, L. (1994). Interview with Linda Darling-Hammond. *Technos, 3(2),* 6–9.

Davis, F. B. (1942). Two new measures of reading ability. *Journal of Educational Psychology, 33,* 365–372.

Dede, C. (Ed.). (1998). Learning with technology. In *1998 ASCD yearbook.* Alexandria, VA: Association for Supervision and Curriculum Development.

Department of Education [New Zealand]. (1985). *Reading in junior classes.* Wellington, New Zealand: Department of Education.

Dewey, J. (1938). *Experience and education.* New York: Macmillan.

Dhority, L. F., & Jensen, E. (1998). *Joyful fluency: Brain-compatible second language acquisition.* San Diego, CA: The Brain Store.

Diamond, M., & Hopson, J. (1998). *Magic trees of the mind.* New York: Dutton.

Dickinson, D. K., & Smith, M. W. (1994). Long-term effects of preschool teachers' book readings on low-income children's vocabulary and story comprehension. *Reading Research Quarterly, 29,* 105–122.

Dowhower, S. L. (1999). Supporting a strategic stance in the classroom: A comprehension framework for helping teachers help students to be strategic. In International Reading Association (Eds.), *Evidence-based reading instruction: Putting the national reading panel report into practice.* Newark, DE: International Reading Association.

Duffelmeyer, F. A. (1980). The influence of experience-based vocabulary instruction on learning word meanings. *Journal of Reading, 24,* 35–40.

Dunston, P. J. (1992). A critique of graphic organizer research. *Reading Research and Instruction, 31*(2), 57–65.

Fiske, E. B. (1983, September 8). Americans in electronic era are reading as much as ever. *New York Times,* p. 1.

Fountas, I. C., & Pinnell, G. S. (1996). *Guided reading: Good first teaching for all children.* Portsmouth, NH: Heinemann.

Fry, E. (1999). *1000 instant words.* Westminster, CA: Teacher Created Materials.

Gallagher, K. (2003). *Reading reasons: Motivational mini-lessons for middle and high school.* Portland, ME: Stenhouse.

Gardiner, M. (1996). Learning improved by arts training. *Scientific Correspondence in Nature, 381,* 284.

Gardner, H. (1983). *Frames of mind. The theory of multiple intelligences.* New York: Basic Books.

Gibbs, J. (2001). *Tribes: A new way of learning and being together.* Windsor, CA: Center Source Systems.

Glynn, S. (1996). Teaching with analogies: Building on the science textbook. *The Reading Teacher, 49,* 490–492.

Goodman, K. S. (1996). *Reading strategies; focus on comprehension.* Katonah, NY: Richard C. Owen.

Gough, P. B. (1972). One second of reading. In J. F. Kavanagh & I. G. Mattingly (Eds.), *Language by ear and by eye* (pp. 331–358).

Gregory, G., & Chapman, C. (2002). *Differentiated instructional strategies: One size doesn't fit all.* Thousand Oaks, CA: Corwin Press.

Guglielmino, L. M. (1986). The affective edge: Using songs and music in ESL instruction. *Adult Literacy and Basic Education, 10,* 19–26.

Gunning, T. G. (1996). Creating reading instruction for all children (2nd ed.). Boston: Allyn and Bacon.

Gwynne, F. (1970). *The king who rained.* New York: Half Moon Books.

Hadwin, A., Kirby, J., & Woodhouse, R. (1999). Individual differences in note-taking, summarization, and learning from lectures. *Alberta Journal of Educational Research, 45,* 1–17.

Hannaford, C. (1995). *Smart moves: Why learning is not all in your head.* Arlington. VA: Great Oceans.

Hansen, J., & Hubbard, R. (1984). Poor readers can draw inferences. *The Reading Teacher, 37,* 586–589.

Harris, T. L., & Hodges, R. E. (1995). *The literacy dictionary: The vocabulary of reading and writing.* Newark, DE: International Reading Association.

Harris, V. J. (1990). African-American children's literature: The first one hundred years. *Journal of Negro Education, 59,* 540–555.

Harvey, S., & Goudvis, A. (2000). *Strategies that work: Teaching comprehension to enhance learning.* York, ME: Stenhouse.

Healy, J. M. (1998). *Failure to connect: How computers affect our children's minds—for better or worse.* Simon & Schuster.

Heckelman, R. G. (1969). A neurological impress method of reading instruction. *Academic Therapy, 4,* 277–282.

Hirsch, E. D., Jr. (2003). Reading comprehension requires knowledge and words and the world. *American Educator, 27(1),* 10–22, 28–29, 48.

Holloway, J. H. (2000). The digital divide. *Educational Leadership, 58,* 90.

Ihnot, C. (2005). *Read Naturally* [online]. Retrieved from http://www.readnaturally.com.

Isaacson, A. (1987). A fingerspelling approach to spelling. *Academic Therapy, 23,* 89–90.

Jackson, F. R. (1998). Seven strategies to support a culturally responsive pedagogy. In International Reading Association (Eds.), *Literacy instruction for culturally and linguistically diverse students* (pp. 57–63). Newark, DE: International Reading Association.

Jensen, E. (1997). *Brain-compatible strategies.* San Diego, CA: The Brain Store.

Jensen, E. (2000). Moving with the brain in mind. *Educational Leadership, 58(3),* 34–37.

Jensen, E. (2001). *Arts with the brain in mind.* Alexandria, VA: Association for Supervision and Curriculum Development.

Johnson, D. W., Johnson, R. T., & Holubeck, E. J. (1990). *Cooperation in the classroom.* Edina, MN: Interaction Books.

Joseph, L. M. (1999). Word boxes help children with learning disabilities identify and spell words. In International Reading Association (Eds.), *Evidence-based reading instruction: Putting the national reading panel into practice* (pp. 23–31). Newark, DE: International Reading Association.

Keene, E. O., & Zimmermann, S. (1997). *Mosaic of thought: Teaching comprehension in a reader's workshop.* Portsmouth: NH. Heinemann.

Killion, J. (2003). Use these 6 keys to open doors to literacy: Study of what works by NSDC and NEA distills principles for success. *Journal of the National Staff Development Council, 24*(2), 10–16.

Klingner, J. K., & Vaughn, S. (1999). Promoting reading comprehension, content learning, and English acquisition through collaborative strategic reading (CSR). In International Reading Association (Eds.), *Evidence-based reading instruction: Putting the national reading panel report into practice* (pp. 222–231). Newark, DE: International Reading Association.

Kuse, L. S., & Kuse, H. R. (1986). Using analogies to study social studies texts. *Social Education, 50,* 24–25.

Laframboise, K. L. (2000). Teaching reading: Said webs: Remedy for tired words. In International Reading Association (Eds.), *Evidence-based reading instruction: Putting the national reading panel report into practice* (pp. 127–129). Newark, DE: International Reading Association.

Linn, M. C., & Slotta, J. D. (2000). WISE science. *Educational Leadership, 58,* 29–32.

Luongo-Orlando, K. (2001). *A project approach to language learning.* Markham, Canada: Pembroke.

Lyon, R., & Fletcher, J. M. (2001). Early warning systems. *Education Matters* [online]. Retrieved June 6, 2001, from http://www.edmatters.org/20012/22.html

Markowitz, K., & Jensen, E. (1999). *The great memory book.* San Diego, CA: The Brain Store.

Martinez, M., Roser, N. L., & Strecker, S. (2002). "I never thought I could be a star": A readers theatre ticket to fluency. In International Reading Association (Eds.), *Evidence-based reading instruction: Putting the national reading panel report into practice.* Newark, DE: International Reading Association.

Marzano, R. J., Gaddy, B. B., & Dean, C. (2000). *What works in classroom instruction.* Aurora, CO: Mid-continent Research for Education and Learning.

Marzano, R. J., Pickering, D. J., & Pollack, J. E. (2001). *Classroom instruction that works.* Alexandria, VA: Association for Supervision and Curriculum Development.

Marzano, R., & Marzano, J. (1988). *A cluster approach to vocabulary instruction.* Newark, DE: International Reading Association.

Mattingly, I. (1984). Reading, linguistic awareness, and language acquisition. In J. Downing & R. Valtin (Eds.), *Language awareness and learning to read* (pp. 9–25). New York: Springer-Verlag.

McCarthy, B. (1990). Using the 4MAT system to bring learning styles to schools. *Educational Leadership, 48*(2), 31–37.

McEwan, E. K. (2001). *Raising reading achievement in middle and high schools: 5 simple-to-follow strategies for principals.* Thousand Oaks, CA. Corwin Press.

McEwan, E. K. (2004). *7 strategies of highly effective readers: Using cognitive research to boost K–8 achievement.* Thousand Oaks, CA: Corwin Press.

Miller, D. (2002). *Reading with meaning: Teaching comprehension in the primary grades.* Portland, ME: Stenhouse.

Moats, L. C. (1998). Teaching decoding. *American Educator, 22*(1–2), 42-49, 95–96.

Moline, S. (1995). *I see what you mean: Children at work with visual information.* York, ME: Stenhouse.

Nagy, W. E. (1988). *Teaching vocabulary to improve reading comprehension.* Newark, DE: International Reading Association.

National Center for Education Statistics. (1999). Executive Summary. In *NAEP 1998 report card for the nation and the states.* Washington, DC: Author, U. S. Department of Education.

National Council of Teachers of English (NCTE) and International Reading Association (IRA). (1996). *Standards for the English Language Arts.* Urbana, IL: NCTE; Newark, DE: IRA.

National Reading Panel. (2000). *Report of the National Reading Panel: Teaching children to read: An evidence based assessment of the scientific research literature on reading and its implications for reading instruction.* Washington, DC: National Institute of Child Health and Development.

Nicholson, T. (1991). Do children read words better in context or in lists? A classic study revisited. *Journal of Educational Psychology, 83,* 444–450.

Norton, D. E. (1990). Teaching multicultural literature in the reading curriculum. In M. F. Opitz (Ed.), *Literacy instruction for culturally and linguistically diverse students* (pp. 213–228). Newark, DE: International Reading Association.

Ogle, D. M. (2000). Make it visual: A picture is worth a thousand words. In M. McLaughlin & M. Vogt (Eds.), *Creativity and innovation in content area teaching.* Norwood, MA: Christopher-Gordon.

Parry, T., & Gregory, G. (1998). *Designing brain-compatible learning.* Arlington Heights, IL: Skylight.

Partnership for Reading. (2001). *Put reading first: The research building blocks for teaching children to read.* Washington, DC: National Institute for Literacy.

Pert, C. (1997). *Molecules of emotion. Why you feel the way you feel.* New York: Scribner.

Petrosky, A. R. (1980). The inferences we make: Children and literature. *Language Arts, 57,* 149–156.

Pinnell, G. S., & Fountas, I. C. (2004). *Sing a song of poetry: A teaching resource for phonemic awareness, phonics, and fluency.* Portsmouth, NH: FirstHand.

Pinnell, G. S., Pikulski, J. J., Wixson, K. K., Compbell, J. R., Gough, P. B., & Beatty, A. S. (1995). *Listening to children read aloud.* Washington, DC: Office of Educational Research and Improvement, U.S. Department of Education.

Powell, R. G. (1998). Johnny can't talk, either: The perpetuation of the deficit theory in classrooms. In M. F. Opitz (Ed.), *Literacy instruction for culturally and linguistically diverse students* (pp. 21–26). Newark, DE: International Reading Association.

Rasinski, T. V. (2003). *The fluent reader: Oral reading strategies for building word recognition, fluency, and comprehension.* New York: Scholastic Professional Books.

Rasinski, T. V., & Padak, N. D. (2001). *From phonics to fluency: Effective teaching of decoding and reading fluency in the elementary school.* New York: Addison Wesley Longman.

Revenaugh, M. (2000). Toward a 24/7 learning community. *Educational Leadership, 58,* 25–28.

Robbins, C., & Ehri, L. C. (1994). Reading storybooks to kindergarteners helps them learn new vocabulary words. *Journal of Educational Psychology, 86,* 54–64.

Routman, R. (1991). *Invitations: Changing as teachers and learners K–12.* Portsmouth, NH: Heinemann.

Routman, R. (2000). *Conversations: Strategies for teaching, learning, and evaluating.* Portsmouth, NH: Heinemann.

Rupley, W. H., Logan, J. W., & Nichols, W. D. (1999). Vocabulary instruction in a balanced reading program. In International Reading Association (Eds.), *Evidenced-based reading instruction: Putting the national reading panel report into practice* (pp. 114–124). Newark, DE: International Reading Association.

Sanders, W., & Rivers, J. (1996). *Cumulative and residual effects of teachers on future student academic achievement.* Knoxville: University of Tennessee Value-Added Research and Assessment Center.

Scharer, P. L. (1992). Teachers in transition: An exploration of changes in teachers and classrooms during implementation of literature-based reading instruction. *Research in the Teaching of English, 26,* 408–445.

Secretary's Commission on Achieving Necessary Skills. (1991). *What work requires of schools: A SCANS report for America 2000.* Washington, DC: U.S. Department of Labor.

Share, D. L., & Stanovich, K. E. (1995). Cognitive processes in early reading development: Accommodating individual differences into a mode of acquisition. *Issues in Education: Contributions from Educational Psychology, 1,* 1–57.

Silver, H. F., Strong, R. W., & Perini, M. J. (2001). *Tools for promoting active in-depth learning* (2nd ed.). Trenton, NJ: Thoughtful Education Press.

Sinatra, R., Beaudry, J. S., Stahl-Gemake, J., & Guastello, E. F. (1990). In M. F. Opitz (Ed.), *Literacy instruction for culturally and linguistically diverse students* (pp. 173–179). Newark, DE: International Reading Association.

Smith, J., & Elley, W. (1997). *How children learn to read.* Katonah, NY: Richard C. Owen.

Snow, C. E., Burns, M. S., & Griffin, P. (Eds.) 1998. *Preventing reading difficulties in young children.* Washington, DC: National Academy Press.

Society for Developmental Education. (1995). *Pyramid of learning.* Peterborough, NH: Author.

Sousa, D. (1995). *How the brain learns: A classroom teacher's guide.* Reston, VA: National Association of Secondary School Principals.

Sprenger, M. (1999). *Learning and memory: The brain in action.* Alexandria, VA: Association for Supervision and Curriculum Development.

Stahl, S. S. (1992). Saying the "p" word: Nine guidelines for exemplary phonics instruction. In International Reading Association (Eds.), *Evidence-based reading instruction: Putting the national reading panel report into practice* (pp. 61–68). Newark, DE: International Reading Association.

Stauffer, R. G. (1975). *Directing the direct reading-thinking process.* New York: Harper & Row.

Sternberg, R. J., & Grigorenko, E. L. (2000). *Teaching for successful intelligence: To increase student learning and achievement.* Arlington Heights, IL: Skylight.

Storm, B. (1999). The enhanced imagination: Storytelling? Power to entrance listeners. *Storytelling, 2*(2).

Strickland, D. S. (1998). Principles of instruction. In M. F. Opitz (Ed.), *Literacy Instruction for Culturally and Linguistically Diverse Students* (pp. 173-179). Newark, DE: International Reading Association.

Strong, R. W., Silver, H. F., Perini, M. J., & Tuculescu, G. M. (2002). *Reading for academic success: Powerful strategies for struggling, average, and advanced readers, Grades 7–12.* Thousand Oaks, CA: Corwin Press.

Sutton, C. (1998). Helping the nonnative English speaker with reading. In M. F. Opitz (Ed.), *Literacy instruction for culturally and linguistically diverse students* (pp. 81–86). Newark, DE: International Reading Association.

Tanner, M. L., & Cassados, L. (1998). Writing to learn. In J. Irwin & M. Doyle (Eds.), *Reading/writing connections: Learning from research* (pp.145–159). Newark, DE: International Reading Association.

Tate, M. L. (2003). *Worksheets don't grow dendrites: 20 instructional strategies that engage the brain.* Thousand Oaks, CA: Corwin Press.

Teele, S. (2004). *Overcoming barricades to reading: A multiple intelligences approach.* Thousand Oaks, CA: Corwin Press.

Tomlinson, T. (1992). *Hard work and high expectations: Motivating students to learn.* Washington, DC: U. S. Department of Education Office of Research and Improvement.

Topping, K. (1995). *Paired reading, spelling, and writing.* New York: Cassell.

Towell, J. (1998, January) Fun with vocabulary. In International Reading Association (Eds.), *Evidence-based reading instruction: Putting the national reading panel report into practice* (pp. 134–136). Newark, DE: International Reading Association.

Uchida, M. C., Cetron, M., & McKenzie, F. (1996). *Preparing students for the 21st century.* Arlington, VA: American Association of School Administrators.

Vacca, J. L., Vacca, R. T., Gove, M. K., Burkey, L., Lenhart, L. A., & McKeon, C. (2003). *Reading and learning to read* (5th ed.). Boston: Allyn & Bacon.

Westwater, A., & Wolfe, P. (2000). The brain-compatible curriculum. *Educational Leadership, 58*(3), 49–52.

Wiggins, G., & McTighe, J. (1998). *Understanding by design.* Alexandria, VA: Association for Supervision and Curriculum Development.

Wolfe, P., & Nevills, P. (2004). *Building the reading brain, PreK–3.* Thousand Oaks, CA: Corwin Press.

Yokota, J. (1993). Issues in selecting multicultural children's literature. In M. F. Opitz (Ed.), *Literacy instruction for culturally and linguistically diverse students* (pp. 184–197). Newark, DE: International Reading Association.

Yopp, H. K. (1995). A test for assessing phonemic awareness in young children. *The Reading Teacher, 49,* 20–29.

Yopp, R. H., & Yopp, H. K. (2000). Sharing informational text with young children. In International Reading Association (Eds.), *Evidence- based reading instruction: Putting the national reading panel report into practice* (pp. 193–206). Newark, DE: International Reading Association.

Young, T. A., & Ferguson, P. M. (1998). From Anansi to Zomo: Trickster tales in the classroom. In International Reading Association (Eds.), *Literacy instruction for culturally and linguistically diverse students* (pp. 258–274). Newark, DE: International Reading Association.

Zarnowski, M. (1995, Summer). Learning history with informational storybooks: A social studies educator's perspective. *The New Advocate,* 188.

Index

CORWIN PRESS

The Corwin Press logo—a raven striding across an open book—represents the union of courage and learning. Corwin Press is committed to improving education for all learners by publishing books and other professional development resources for those serving the field of K–12 education. By providing practical, hands-on materials, Corwin Press continues to carry out the promise of its motto: **"Helping Educators Do Their Work Better."**